# Racially Biased Policing

# Racially Biased Policing: A Principled Response

*Lorie Fridell, Robert Lunney,*
*Drew Diamond and Bruce Kubu*

*with Michael Scott and Colleen Laing*

POLICE EXECUTIVE
RESEARCH FORUM

The research reported here was conducted through the Police Executive Research Forum and funded by the Office of Community Oriented Policing Services under grant 1999-CK-WX-0076. The points of view expressed here are those of the authors and do not necessarily represent the official position of the Office of Community Oriented Policing Services or the Police Executive Research Forum or its members.

Police Executive Research Forum, Washington, D.C. 20036

Published 2001.

Printed in the United States of America

Library of Congress Number 01-132420
ISBN 1-878734-73-3

Cover art by Kittner Design
Interior design by Elliot Thomas Grant, etg Design

# Contents

# Acknowledgments

The PERF project team is especially grateful to the Office of Community Oriented Policing Services (COPS Office) for determining the need for this undertaking, and for providing both funding and guidance. Particular thanks go to Ellen Scrivner, deputy director, who served as our project monitor. She was actively involved in the project at all stages, providing much-valued ideas, guidance and support. We are grateful to previous COPS Office directors Joe Brann and Tom Frazier, and to Acting Director Ralph Justus, for their vital support. We also extend our thanks to Tamara Clark for her characteristically professional assistance in attending to the seemingly endless details involved.

We also express our great appreciation to the project advisory board, who provided able guidance to the project team. This group comprised a diverse group of law enforcement practitioners, community activists, civil rights leaders, and academics. We brought this group together to be sure that we heard and considered all competing viewpoints. The recommendations herein are not necessarily endorsed by each individual member of this group: Lynn Bataglia, U.S. Attorney's Office, Baltimore; Chief David Bejarano, San Diego Police Department; the Rev. Jeffery Brown, Union Baptist Church, Cambridge, Mass.; Commissioner Patrick Carroll, New Rochelle (N.Y.) Police Department; John Crew, ACLU of Northern California; Richard Green, Crown Heights Youth Collective, Brooklyn, N.Y.; Colonel Charles Hall, Florida Highway Patrol; J. Howard Henderson, Baltimore Urban League; Pat Hoven, Corporate Community Partnerships; Chief Harold Hurtt, Phoenix Police Department; Deborah Jeon, ACLU of Maryland; Chief Jerry

Oliver, Richmond (Va.) Police Department; Chief Robert Olson, Minneapolis Police Department; Richard Roberts, International Union of Police Associations; Annette Sandberg, former chief, Washington State Patrol; Robert Stewart, National Organization of Black Law Enforcement Executives; and Samuel Walker, University of Nebraska-Omaha.

We extend our thanks to the more than 1,000 law enforcement executives who responded to our survey, many of whom forwarded department materials for our review and consideration. We thank, as well, other practitioners around the nation who forwarded materials to us or called us with input, ideas and advice. We very much appreciate the insights provided to us by the citizens and sworn personnel from across the country who participated in the project focus groups. Their input was critical to identifying the key issues, as well as to developing the proposed agency responses.

In addition, we extend our appreciation to subject-matter experts from around the country whom the authors engaged in discussions or who reviewed and provided valuable input on drafts of various chapters. These experts include sworn police personnel, constitutional scholars, law enforcement counsel, academics, and civil rights activists. While we will not name them all here, particular thanks go to Chief Larry Austin, professor David Carter, Sgt. Don Grinder, professor David Harris, Richard Jerome, Chief Gil Kerlikowske, professor Robert McNamara, Assistant Chief Timothy Oettmeier, Mark Posner, professor Margo Schlanger, Dennis Slocumb, Deputy Chief Mark Spurrier, Detective Clarence Woody, and Alicia Zatcoff. These individuals do not necessarily endorse the recommendations herein.

We are also very grateful to Martha Plotkin and David Edelson of PERF for their able, patient and professional assistance in editing and producing this document. We thank Jim Burack and Rebecca Neuburger of PERF for reviewing chapters and for overseeing the development of the project website, respectively. Suzanne Fregly greatly improved the document with her able editing. Finally, we express our appreciation to Chuck Wexler of PERF for his ongoing support, guidance and leadership.

# Foreword

The vast majority of law enforcement officers—of all ranks, nationwide—are dedicated men and women committed to serving all citizens with fairness and dignity. The Police Executive Research Forum (PERF) shares their intolerance for racially biased policing, and hopes *Racially Biased Policing: A Principled Response* will enhance citizen and police efforts to detect and eradicate it. Addressing racially biased policing, and the perceptions of its practice, involve complex issues and challenges. PERF members and their colleagues need to effectively allocate their limited agency resources to address the problem. PERF, with funding and guidance from the Department of Justice's Office of Community Oriented Policing Services, has prepared this report to assist agencies in meeting this challenge. This report is meant to provide the first step in assisting progressive police professionals—in partnership with citizens—to seriously consider the issues and develop approaches tailored to their community's unique needs. It guides law enforcement professionals in their response to racially biased policing and, equally important, to the perceptions of its practice, to strengthen citizen confidence in the police and improve services to all our communities.

The issues involved in "racial profiling" and racially biased policing are not new—they are the latest manifestation of a long history of sometimes tense, and even volatile, police-minority relations. This need not be viewed, however, as proof of the problem's intractability. Police are more capable than ever of effectively addressing police racial bias. In the past few decades, there has been a revolution in the quality and quantity of police training, the standards for hiring officers, the procedures and accountability regarding police activity, and the widespread adoption of community policing.

There is no single cure for the problems underlying racially biased policing, and you will not find any definitive one here. This report summarizes some of the latest thinking and efforts across the nation regarding this difficult problem. PERF used many sources to develop the recommendations contained in this report. We conducted a national survey of more than 1,000 agency executives, reviewed the materials of more than 250 agencies, spoke with citizens and practitioners in a series of focus groups held around the country, conducted a literature review, and conferred with subject-matter experts in various topic areas. PERF also integrated comments from discussions among chiefs at PERF national meetings. In addition, this project greatly benefited from the guidance of an advisory board composed of respected law enforcement agency executives, Justice Department personnel, community activists, and civil rights leaders.

These sources helped PERF identify six key response areas: department accountability and supervision, policy, recruitment and hiring, education and training, minority community outreach, and data collection. PERF believes important and meaningful changes can occur within each of these areas. Of course, the contents of this report cannot allay long-standing police-minority tensions. Clearly, resolving racial bias in law enforcement, as in society at large, will require long-term dedication and innovation. We hope this report will help agencies continue on that path.

There are key themes underlying the recommendations we have developed. First, racially biased policing is at its core a human rights issue. While some may view it as merely a public relations problem, a political issue or an administrative challenge, in the final analysis, racially biased policing is antithetical to democratic policing. Protecting individual rights is not an *inconvenience* for modern police; it is the *foundation* of policing in a democratic society. Second, racially biased policing is not solely a "law enforcement problem," but rather a problem that can be solved only through police-citizen partnerships based on mutual trust and respect. We provide guidance for forming such partnerships in this report. Third, police personnel around the country *want* to respond effectively to local and national concerns regarding racially biased policing. It is to these personnel that we dedicate this report. We must support their efforts to address racially biased policing and, in so doing, help them serve, protect and defend *all* citizens with the highest professional values and standards.

We will surely benefit from the experience of departments that translate the recommendations we provide into action, and from the new ideas generated in the process. We hope this report will advance the approaches to and national debate on racially biased policing. The result will be a fair and dignified system of justice for us all.

Chuck Wexler
*PERF Executive Director*

# Critical Issues in
# Racially Biased Policing

## INTRODUCTION

American policing is facing a tremendous challenge—a widespread perception that the police are routinely guilty of bias in how they treat racial minorities. This comes at a time when crime rates have fallen almost everywhere in recent years, and when the police might otherwise be celebrating their contribution to reducing crime and creating safe communities. Instead, the police find themselves baffled and defensive.

Racial and ethnic minorities constitute a substantial and growing segment of the U.S. population. Strength is in diversity, and we look to minority communities to participate fully in all aspects of society. Police are now looking to the public for partnerships and collaborative problem-solving solutions to community ills. If substantial segments of the community are the victims of police bias, or even perceive that they are, the likelihood of success is dim. We all know that racial profiling is unacceptable and is at variance with the standards and values inherent in ensuring fair and dignified police response to all. We believe that the vast majority of law enforcement in this country are hard-working men and women who are committed to serving all members of our communities with equity and dignity. Yet the challenges of addressing racially biased policing, and perceptions thereof, clearly indicate that police must do more to address the concerns of minority citizens.

The Police Executive Research Forum (PERF), with funding from the Office of Community Oriented Policing Services, developed this report as a reference to help police leaders respond to the issues associated with racial profiling. The acknowledgments attest to the extensive participation of police leaders, academics, civil rights activists and others.

## THE STORIES

Many minorities believe that the police routinely stop and search them because of their skin color. The evidence of this belief is found first in "stories," and the stories are legion. Many of these recounted tales ring with authenticity; they are compelling and devastating in their impact on people's lives. Racial bias distorts attitudes toward civil authority and the police, and blights the quality of everyday life. In addition to actual bias, a strong and ingrained perception of bias is a substantial barrier to full enjoyment of freedom and civil rights. It colors every aspect of life for minorities. At its root, bias is a denial of justice.

These are accounts of people who have been stopped by police on questionable grounds and subjected to disrespectful behavior, intrusive questioning and disregard for their civil rights. The storytellers come from all walks of life: they are young men and women, the elderly, people from the middle and upper classes, professional athletes, lawyers, doctors, and police officers at every rank.

This is how it goes:

- A young black woman, in desperation, finally trades her new sports car for an older model because police have repeatedly stopped her on suspicion of possession of a stolen vehicle.
- An elderly African-American couple returning from a social event in formal dress are stopped and questioned at length, allegedly because their car resembles one identified in a robbery.
- A prominent black lawyer driving a luxury car is frequently stopped on various pretexts.

- A Hispanic deputy police chief is stopped numerous times in neighboring jurisdictions, apparently on "suspicion."
- A young Hispanic man working evening shift drives home on the same route five nights a week after midnight, and is stopped for suspicious behavior almost every night.
- A black judge far removed from her home jurisdiction is stopped, handcuffed and laid facedown on the pavement while police search her car. They issue no citations.

According to recent national surveys, the majority of white, as well as black, Americans say that racial profiling is widespread in the United States today. Law enforcement executives need to reflect seriously on this and respond to both the reality of, and the perceptions of, biased policing. This chapter provides a context for defining the issues, and previews our recommendations for an effective response.

## ISSUE DEFINITION

We have chosen to avoid the term "racial profiling" and, instead, refer to "racially biased policing." We believe "racial profiling" has frequently been defined so restrictively that it does not fully capture the concerns of both police practitioners and citizens. For instance, racial profiling is frequently defined as law enforcement activities (e.g., detentions, arrests, searches) that are initiated *solely* on the basis of race. Central to the debate on the most frequently used definitions is the word "solely." In the realm of potential discriminatory actions, this definition likely references only a very small portion. Even a racially prejudiced officer likely uses more than the single factor of race when conducting biased law enforcement. For example, officers might make decisions based on the neighborhood *and* the race of the person, the age of the car *and* the race of the person, or the gender *and* the race of the person. Activities based on these sample pairs of factors would fall outside the most commonly used definition of racial profiling.

Moreover, one could interpret the common definition of racial profiling to not include activities that are legally supportable in terms of reasonable suspicion or probable cause, but are nonetheless racially biased. As above, a definition that prohibits enforcement decisions based "solely" on race would not encompass decisions based on reasonable suspicion or probable cause plus race. That is, this definition could be interpreted to exclude, for instance, officers' pulling over black traffic violators and not white, or citing Hispanic, but not white, youth for noise violations. Such disparate treatment would not necessarily be encompassed by a definition that referred to actions based "solely" on race, because the officers would have acted on the basis of reasonable suspicion or probable cause, as well as race.

In addition, using the word "profiling" to address the issue of bias not only creates confusion about an otherwise legitimate policing term, but also semantically limits the potential abuse to those instances in which an officer might use race as an indicator of criminal activity. While, indeed, this is a major concern and likely where the greatest potential for abuse lies, departments wish to prohibit biased law enforcement that is based not only on stereotypes regarding the link between race and crime, but also on other negative attitudes regarding race. For instance, an officer may be prejudiced against ethnic minorities and stop them for purposes of harassment, independent of any notion that their race is an indicator of criminal activity. The narrowest definitions of "racial profiling" refer to police activities in the context only of *vehicle stops*, ignoring the potential for police abuse of power in the many other activities in which they engage citizens.

Most importantly, during the course of this project, it became clear that the term "racial profiling" hampered the national discussion of the problem. This was most clearly exemplified in project focus groups composed of both police and citizens. Project staff noted that most *citizens* were using the term "racial profiling" to discuss *all* manifestations of racial bias in policing. The *police* participants were likely to define "racial profiling" quite narrowly—as law enforcement activities (particularly vehicle stops) based *solely* on race. The citizens claimed that "racial profiling," as they defined it, was widespread. In contrast, the police, using their more narrow definition, were frequently quite adamant that police activities based solely on race were quite rare. These contrasting, but unspoken, definitions lead to police defensiveness and citizen frustration.

We found that citizens and police can have constructive conversation on the topic of "racially biased policing." This term more accurately reflects the concerns expressed by citizens, and few police officers would deny that some officers are influenced by personal bias in performing their duties, whatever the motivation.

Racially biased policing occurs when law enforcement inappropriately considers race or ethnicity in deciding with whom and how to intervene in an enforcement capacity. Racially biased policing is defined and interpreted through the policy outlined in Chapter 4.

Racially biased policing and the perceptions thereof are the themes of this report. We hope the recommendations and guidance will facilitate an effective law enforcement response to both of these important issues. The report focuses only on racially biased policing, although some recommendations could apply to situations in which gender, age, economic status, or sexual preference are at issue.

## BALANCE IN THE CAUSE OF JUSTICE

In charters and legislation across the country, we find primacy given to the role of the police as enforcers of the law. While law enforcement is undeniably essential to maintaining good government, policing in a democratic society demands more. The police are essential to the fabric of society, not only as enforcers of first resort for federal, state and local laws, but also as moderators of behavior, keepers of the public peace and agents of prevention. Increasingly, police are recognized for their capacity for community problem-solving, collaborating with a broad range of citizen groups, individuals and institutional partners to improve the quality of life. Law enforcement remains a prime responsibility, but as a means for attaining the goals of justice and the good of society, and not as an end in itself. Recognition of this principle is a shared responsibility of police, government and the community. Failure to achieve a balance in police priorities creates misunderstanding and mis-direction.

There are grave dangers in neglecting to take the issue of biased policing seriously and respond with effective initiatives. Societal division on racial grounds will leach the vigor from quality-of-life initiatives, regardless of how well-intended and well-funded. If a substantial part of the population comes to view the justice system as unjust, they are less likely to be co-operative with police, withholding participation in community problem-solving and demonstrating their disaffection in a va-riety of ways. The loss of moral authority could do permanent injury to the legal system, and deprive all of society of the pro-tection of the law.

## PROGRAM FOR ACTION

This report provides assistance to agencies so they may take responsibility for addressing the important issues of racially biased policing and the perceptions thereof. It is divided into six areas in which action is needed:

- accountability and supervision,
- policies prohibiting biased policing,
- recruitment and hiring,
- education and training,
- minority community outreach, and
- data collection and analysis.

### Accountability and Supervision

Police accountability and supervision are important factors in reducing or eliminating bias in policing. The tasks of po-licing are most often performed by single officers or pairs of officers operating independently and without immediate in-stitutional oversight or independent observers. Under these circumstances, accountability is difficult to ensure. One ver-dict appears clear from the most recent controversies regard-ing police misconduct: The "bad apple" analogy is no longer resonating as the only credible explanation. Increasingly, organizational culture is recognized as the most important factor influencing police behavior. Enlightened police leaders have learned that influencing the culture may be the most effective means of deterring bias and pursuing the goals of quality policing.

The chapter on accountability and supervision addresses human rights, a core value of policing in a democratic society. Indeed, if we were to suggest a single focus for ameliorating the many problems surrounding the topic of biased policing, it would be to influence recognition of the centrality of human rights in the broadest sense. In addition, we provide recommendations for maintaining quality assurance, valuing diversity and managing public complaints. We discuss the roles and responsibilities of middle managers and supervisors, and include proposals for consideration.

## Policies Prohibiting Biased Policing

Police policy gives direction and authority to mission and value statements. Procedures provide the operating details to guide personnel in conducting their duties. Policies and procedures are critical to achieving agency goals. In the wake of current events related to "racial profiling," police departments across the nation have adopted policies prohibiting "racial profiling." These policies represent an important effort to convey to both citizens and police that "racial profiling" will not be tolerated. Unfortunately, the vast majority of these policies do little to clarify how officers can conduct their activities in a racially neutral way (albeit some agencies may address this in training). Of particular concern is the lack of guidance that we provide officers with regard to whether and how they can use race as one factor in a set of factors to establish reasonable suspicion or probable cause and to make other law enforcement decisions. In this report, we propose a policy for agencies that addresses both racially biased policing and the perceptions thereof, and provide guidance to officers on using race as a factor in law enforcement decisions.

## Recruitment and Hiring

In terms of recruitment and selection, police agencies have the potential to reduce racial bias by hiring officers who can police in an unbiased way, and by hiring a workforce that reflects the community's racial demographics. Communities expect their police officers to carry out their duties with fairness, integrity, diligence, and impartiality. Police agencies must ensure they recruit the best-suited women and men to meet these expectations. In developing a workforce that reflects the diversity of the community served, an agency conveys a sense of fairness and equity to the public; increases the probability that, as a whole, the agency will be able to understand the perspectives of its racial minorities and communicate effectively with them; and increases the likelihood that officers will come to better understand and respect various racial and cultural perspectives through their daily interactions with community members. In this report, we discuss police recruitment and hiring as they relate to the issue of biased policing, providing recommendations for police-community initiatives.

## Education and Training

Education and training are essential components of a comprehensive strategy to reduce racially biased policing and perceptions thereof. They can be used to convey new information, provide and refine critical skills, encourage compliance with policies and rules, facilitate dialogue, and/or convey a commitment to addressing the problem. Programs can target citizens, as well as the police, and should be tailored to the particular needs, concerns and experiences of the local agency and community. A key theme to be conveyed to both academy and in-service practitioners is that respect for human rights is a central and affirmative part of the police mission. Within this context, police can benefit from understanding the dimensions, complexities and subtleties of racially biased policing, as well as the impact of these types of activities on individual citizens, the department and the community. Police should receive specific guidance regarding whether and how race can be used to make decisions and reflect upon not only officer-level decisions, but precinct- or department-level decisions that may manifest racially biased policing. In this report, we discuss these priority topics for police training and successful methods for conveying them.

## Minority Community Outreach

In the absence of strong functional links to community groups and local institutions, the police mission will likely fail. Grave damage is inflicted on police-community relationships when the police become consciously disengaged from the public. An aloof police agency making decisions motivated by its own self-interest risks alienation that often culminates in violence and disorder. The police hold primary responsibility for community outreach on many levels. The community bears a reciprocal responsibility to respond to opportunities for positive relationships. Policing with the community can function only in an environment of mutual engagement and respect. In the context of the issue we are addressing—racially biased policing—outreach to minority communities is imperative.

This report lists necessary competencies for police agencies seeking to develop and maintain outreach to minority communities, and recommends that agencies form police-citizen task forces to identify how they can effectively respond to the issues of biased policing and the perceptions thereof. We also include a list of contemporary and progressive practices for consideration. To build and sustain relationships reflecting mutual trust and respect is the ultimate objective.

## Data Collection and Analysis

However compelling, anecdotal evidence of racially biased policing is not sufficient to determine the nature and extent of the problem. Progressive policing is committed to accountability and openness, which can be reflected in efforts geared toward self-assessment. Data collection conveys to citizens that the agency will address community concerns.

That said, we caution against an overemphasis on data collection and analysis as the sole or primary methods for responding to the issues of biased policing, and against high expectations regarding their use in producing valid answers to the serious and legitimate questions an agency seeks to answer. In this report, we set forth the positive and negative aspects of data collection and analysis, and encourage agencies to make decisions regarding whether to collect and analyze data in light of agency resources, political factors and other efforts to address racially biased policing. For those that are mandated or choose to collect and analyze data, we provide guidance for developing a data collection and analysis protocol.

## GOVERNMENT SUPPORT

The political system, courts, civilian administrators, and various oversight agencies share responsibility to hold law enforcement—police leaders and individual officers—accountable. While, historically, these accountability mechanisms have functioned unevenly, they remain central to initiating and strengthening any change process. This report focuses on the police, but other parties must be prepared to assume their responsibility. For instance, other government agencies must be prepared to provide support and guidance. Most notably, local, state and federal government must be prepared to provide the financial support police agencies will need to implement the recommendations in this report. Racial distinction is not a problem unique to policing; rather, it is a societal issue for which all government agencies must share responsibility.

Many of the policy and behavioral changes recommended in this report may be achieved at negligible cost, but innovative recruitment and selection initiatives, data collection and analysis, in-car video equipment, curriculum development, and training will be added expenses to police budgets. State or local governments that mandate data collection and analysis and other changes must be prepared to offer financial support.

## CONCLUSION

If prejudice, arbitrary decisions, treatment disparity, and disrespect are to be replaced by universal respect and equitable use of police powers, then we must begin a process of bringing all of policing into accord with democratic principles. We must insist that protection of human rights is a fundamental responsibility of police. We must ensure at all costs the primacy of the rule of law, and scrupulously monitor the use of police authority for compliance. We must carefully examine our beliefs regarding the role of the police, and eradicate from the police culture the mentality that leads to the use of bias in dealing with citizens. We must do this everywhere, and all of the time.

The research and conclusions in this report are meant to further the process of thoughtful, ethically based revision and reform needed to ensure quality policing to all citizens, regardless of race or cultural background. In a society where race is inherently played out in all aspects of life, racially biased policing presents both a challenge and an opportunity for the police to exercise quiet determination and moral leadership, addressing the problem head-on.

# Police and Citizen Perceptions

PERF staff used various data-gathering techniques to collect information for developing recommendations and guidelines regarding the occurrences and perceptions of biased policing. Staff compiled information from informal discussions with various practitioners, subject-matter experts (e.g., law professors and social scientists) and citizens, as well as from several large-scale discussions among police executives at PERF meetings. PERF also conducted focus groups around the nation, and a national survey of police administrators. This chapter describes PERF's key information-gathering methods and results.

## FOCUS GROUPS

Trained facilitators conducted 15 focus groups around the country:[1] three with citizens, four with police line staff, three with police command staff, and two with police executives (one with state chiefs, and the other with local agency chiefs). In addition, we held three focus groups with both citizen and law enforcement participants. The facilitators led discussions on vehicle stops, racial profiling and biased policing. Below we report on some of the key findings from these sessions that informed our recommendations.

---

[1] One focus group was held in New York, one in Virginia, four in Maryland, four in California, and five in Massachusetts.

## Citizen Views

Consistent with national polls, most of the citizens in the groups believed that "racial profiling" occurs. As noted in the previous chapter, their comments indicated a broad definition of the term, encompassing all manifestations of racially biased policing. That is, in describing "racial profiling," these citizens cited a wide range of behaviors, including excessive force against racial and ethnic minorities, as well as illegal stops and rudeness to minorities.

A number of minorities said they are likely to interpret various "negative aspects" of a vehicle stop as racially biased policing. For instance, these participants acknowledged that officer rudeness, discourtesy and/or unwillingness to give the reason for a stop might well be perceived as the result of racial bias as opposed to, for instance, overall (and impartially demonstrated) lack of professionalism.

The "racial profiling" stories the citizens shared made clear the multiplicative impact of negative incidents on citizen trust of police. While some minorities shared their *own* stories of what they perceived to be "racial profiling," virtually *all* the minorities could share stories of incidents involving *other* people. As practitioners well know, people are much more likely to share stories of *negative* police-citizen interactions (regardless of citizen race) than stories of *positive* interactions. Thus, each negative police-citizen interaction has the potential to harm overall police-citizen trust in the jurisdiction.

Overwhelmingly, the participating citizens indicated that, on a vehicle stop, they would like the officer to introduce him- or herself, explain the reason for the stop, be courteous and respectful, and apologize (or at least explain) if a mistake is made (such as on a stop for suspicious circumstances or pursuant to a "Be on the Lookout"). Many of the participating citizens expressed frustration because they perceived that law enforcement was denying the existence of racial profiling.

## Law Enforcement Views

Many of our law enforcement participants *did* express skepticism that "racial profiling" was a major problem, exacerbating some citizens' frustration. It became clear to staff that these differing perceptions among citizens and police regarding racial profiling's pervasiveness were very much related to the respective definitions they had adopted. The citizens equated "racial profiling" with *all* manifestations of racially biased policing, whereas most of the police practitioners defined "racial profiling" as stopping a motorist based *solely* on race. Presumably, even officers who engage in racially biased policing rarely make a vehicle stop based *solely* on race (often ensuring probable cause or some other factor is also present). When the facilitators broadened the discussion by using the term "racially biased policing," police participants were much more likely to acknowledge that a larger problem exists.

Perceptions among law enforcement focus group participants regarding the extent to which either "racial profiling" or "biased policing" exists seemed to vary by officer race. In several of the practitioner focus groups, similar interactions occurred: After a white officer in the group downplayed the scope of the problem, a minority officer would speak up and describe his or her personal experience with being pulled over by police. In several cases, it was clear to the facilitators that white officers were surprised by these stories. Their peers' experiences seemed to impact them in a way that the citizens' stories conveyed in press accounts did not.

Many of the practitioners expressed the belief that, to the extent that racially biased policing occurs, it can be attributed to a small number of rogue officers. It appeared that in jurisdictions where collaboration and trust were good, both the police and citizens were less likely to believe that racial profiling and/or racially biased policing was a major issue.

The facilitators sought views on the definition of "racially biased policing," asking participants to identify, for instance, the circumstances in which officers could use race to make law enforcement decisions. As discussed further in the chapter on policy, even practitioners within the same departments had very different answers to this question.

Officers of all races were united in their great frustration concerning unfounded accusations of all types of bias—including, but not limited to, racial bias. The practitioners remarked, for instance, that citizens might accuse officers of pulling them over on a vehicle stop because they were black, female, Jewish, driving a red car, and so forth. They lamented that many citizens could come up with many reasons for their being stopped, *other* than the fact that they had just violated a traffic law.

Some of the discussions with the practitioners focused on what happens during a vehicle stop. While virtually all practitioner participants agreed that officers should be courteous and respectful during a stop, opinions differed regarding whether an officer should initiate the stop with an introduction and explanation or with a request for "license and registration." Those supporting the introduction/explanation thought that such communication reduced the tensions otherwise inherent in the stop. Those supporting the request for papers believed they needed to access them before the citizen started arguing over the reason for the stop and refused to supply them.

Officers also expressed their desire that citizens better understood that a vehicle stop can be very dangerous and must be handled as such. It was clear that the practitioners had a heightened awareness of the potential danger of vehicle stops.

### Conclusions and Caveats

Focus groups can be valuable forums for better understanding an issue and various viewpoints related to it. Clearly, however, because focus groups are not as scientifically rigorous as other data collection techniques (e.g., samples are not representative), we cannot necessarily presume that the information shared with us by both citizens and practitioners can be generalized to all citizens and police. To gather additional information regarding this issue, PERF conducted a national survey.

### NATIONAL SURVEY

PERF used a mail survey of police executives to examine various aspects of racially biased policing and the perceptions thereof. Specifically, the purposes of the survey were to (1) identify how departments have responded to racial profiling, (2) identify *effective responses* that could form the basis of our recommendations to the field, and (3) assess the impact of current events related to racial profiling on law enforcement agencies.

## Instrument

The survey of police administrators contained a combination of open-ended and multiple-choice questions and included requests that respondents return with their surveys policies they had adopted, training curricula related to the topic, and data collection instruments and protocol, where applicable. The survey and original cover letter are included as the appendix to this chapter.

The project staff developed the survey, and the advisory board members and other selected police administrators pilot-tested it. All were requested to provide feedback regarding questionnaire content and form. PERF used this feedback to improve and refine the instrument.

## Sample Frame and Sample

Our target group for the survey was state and local law enforcement agencies. We drew the sample from the 2000 National Public Safety Information Bureau National Directory of Law Enforcement Administrators. The total number of state and local agencies in this directory is 13,539.[2] To ensure that departments of varying sizes and types were represented, we used a stratified random sample with disproportionate sampling from each strata. We stratified the population of targeted agencies by department size (as measured by number of sworn officers) and department type (i.e., police department, sheriff's department, state police agency). We randomly selected a sample of 2,251 agencies from this stratified population, as set forth in Table 1 (see next page).

## Data Collection and Entry

PERF first mailed the survey to the 2,251 agencies on Oct. 16, 2000. We sent a cover letter and second copy of the survey to

---

[2] Departments that were excluded before generating the stratified random sample were campus law enforcement, child support law enforcement, tribal law enforcement, airport and harbor law enforcement, conservation law enforcement, federal law enforcement, military law enforcement, and railroad law enforcement.

## Table 1. Number of Departments, Sampled by Type and Size

| Number of Officers | Police Departments | | Sheriff's Departments | | State Police Agencies | | TOTAL | |
|---|---|---|---|---|---|---|---|---|
| | Pop. | Sample | Pop. | Sample | Pop. | Sample | Pop. | Sample |
| 1–49 | 8,968 | 904 (10.1%) | 2,393 | 254 (10.6%) | 0 | 0 | 11,361 | 1,158 (10.2%) |
| 50–249 | 1,134 | 462 (40.7%) | 570 | 231 (40.5%) | 6 | 6 (100%) | 1,710 | 699 (40.9%) |
| 250 or more | 196 | 195 (99.5%) | 160 | 156 (97.5%) | 43 | 43 (100%) | 399 | 394 (98.7%) |
| TOTAL | 10,298 | 1,561 (15.2%) | 3,123 | 641 (20.5%) | 49[3] | 49 (100%) | 13,470 | 2,251 (16.7%) |

[3] The Hawaii State Sheriff's Department handles state law enforcement activities. However, Hawaii does not have a state police agency, per se.

each nonresponding agency on Nov. 7. Finally, we sent a third reminder to nonrespondents on Dec. 16. We received 1,087 completed surveys, resulting in a response rate of 48.3 percent. More than 250 agencies submitted policies, data collection protocol and/or training curricula to aid in developing the recommendations and guidelines.

Of the 1,087 surveys received, 811 (74.6%) were from police departments, 241 (22.2%) from sheriff's departments, and 35 (3.2%) from state police agencies. This reflected response rates, by agency type, of 52 percent for police departments, 37.6 percent for sheriff's departments, and 70 percent for state police agencies.

To verify that respondents are representative of the police population, Table 2 (see next page) compares descriptive analyses of the responding law enforcement agencies and the population. Overall, the departments responding to the survey employ an average of 217 sworn officers. The median number of sworn officers for the sample is 60. This compares with the target population, with an average of 52 and a median of 12. Of the departments responding to the survey, the average population of the jurisdiction is 119,654, with a median of 32,500. This compares with a target population average of 38,350 and a median of 7,500. Those departments that responded, on average, employ more sworn officers than those departments in the population. Similarly, and unsurprisingly, they serve greater numbers of people than those departments in the population. The departments in the sample differ from those in the population because we oversampled larger departments, as their raw numbers in the population were smaller (see row percentages, Table 1). We chose to oversample large jurisdictions because they serve the vast majority of the U.S. population.

We conducted analyses to determine if there were identifiable differences between the responding and nonresponding agencies. We used a one-way analysis of variance to determine if agency size was related to response rates. The analysis results indicate that agency size did not significantly impact response rates ($F = 0.150$, $p = 0.699$).

A chi-square analysis indicated that sheriff's departments were significantly less likely to return surveys than police departments

**Table 2. Number of Sworn Officers Employed by Responding Departments, and Populations Served by Those Agencies**

|  | Number of Officers | | Population of Jurisdiction | |
|---|---|---|---|---|
|  | Population | Sample | Population | Sample |
| Mean | 52 | 217 | 38,350 | 119,654 |
| Median | 12 | 60 | 7,500 | 32,500 |
| Std. Dev. | 426 | 642 | 241,960 | 286,301 |
| Minimum | 1 | 1 | 52 | 154 |
| Maximum | 40,000 | 13,400 | 10,000,000 | 3,501,487 |
| No. of Respondents | 13,470 | 1,087 | 13,474 | 1,053 |
| Missing | 69 | 0 | 65 | 34 |

and state police agencies.[4] The low response from sheriff's departments may be due to the fact that a significant proportion of them do not engage in patrol activities. Although we requested that such agencies return their surveys indicating this so that we could classify them as ineligible, many likely did not do so and, instead, ignored the survey. Anecdotally, this was found to be the case.

One-way analysis of variance followed by chi-square analysis indicated that agencies in the northwestern and southwestern regions were significantly more likely to submit surveys than agencies in the north central, south central, northeastern, and southeastern regions.[5]

## Methodological Caveats

The results presented below reflect responses from a large number of law enforcement executives generally representative of executives nationwide. However, as discussed above, our ability to generalize these results to all executives of local and state law enforcement agencies is limited by the following: (1) fewer than half of the agencies in the sample submitted surveys, (2) larger agencies are overrepresented, (3) sheriff's departments are underrepresented, and (4) agencies in the northwestern and southwestern regions are overrepresented. Further, although our target respondents were the agency executives, it is likely that in some cases, someone other than the executive completed the survey. Thus, we cannot be assured that the results pertaining to opinions and perceptions do, in fact, represent those of all agency executives. However, despite these caveats, it is important to note that the local agencies responding to the survey serve one-quarter of the entire U.S. population served by local agencies, and employ one-third of the sworn personnel. One can comfortably assume that their responses can be generalized to many of their counterparts nationwide.

---

[4] Chi-square value $= 46.811$, df $= 2$, $p = 0.001$

[5] We also tested for interaction effects of (1) department size and region, and (2) department type and department size. The interactions terms increased the predictive ability of the model only slightly.

## Results

As indicated above, a major purpose of the survey was to identify promising agency responses to "racial profiling." Information on agency responses was key to making the recommendations in this report. Particularly valuable were the extensive materials agencies forwarded us (e.g., policies, protocol, curricula) and the information they provided about effective practices both within and outside the agencies (e.g., effective training programs and community outreach efforts).

We also included survey items to assess perceptions of the seriousness of "racial profiling," to weigh the impact of current events related to racial profiling on agencies, and to identify the activities in which agencies have engaged. This section reports our findings for these items. Additional results are reported in the chapters that follow.

Two related survey items attempted to weigh the extent to which administrators perceive racial profiling to be a problem, and their perception of the extent to which their minority citizens believe it to be a problem (see Figure 1). A great challenge

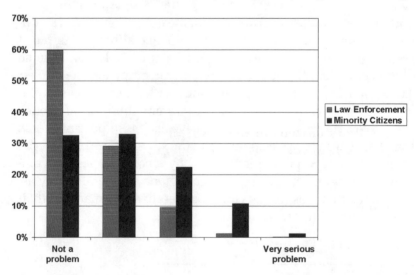

**Fig. 1. Law enforcement executives' perceptions of the degree to which "racial profiling/stereotyping" or racially biased policing is a problem, and their perceptions of the degree to which minority citizens in their jurisdiction think it is a problem**

associated with designing these items related to all of the terminology issues discussed in Chapter 1. Staff wrestled with whether to ask about "racial profiling," "biased policing" or both. Finding no completely satisfactory wording, we chose to include references to both terms. Specifically, one item inquired, "To what extent do *you think* 'racial profiling/stereotyping' or racially biased policing is a problem in your jurisdiction?" and a second inquired, "To what extent do the *racial minority citizens in your jurisdiction* think that 'racial profiling/stereotyping' or biased policing is a problem in your jurisdiction?" The subjects responded using a five-point scale ranging from "not a problem" (1) to "very serious problem" (5). It is important to note that the issues associated with definitions make it difficult to interpret the responses with any precision.

Figure 1 indicates that law enforcement administrators do not believe that "'racial profiling/stereotyping' or racially biased policing" is a serious problem in their jurisdictions, and they believe that the racial minority citizens in their area would generally agree with them. Specifically, a majority of the respondents (59.9%) believe that "'racial profiling/stereotyping' or racially biased policing" is not a problem in their jurisdiction. An additional 29.1 percent perceive racially biased policing to be a minor problem. Only 0.2 percent characterize the problem as "very serious," and an additional 1.2 percent characterize the problem as somewhat serious.

Similarly, one-third (32.6%) of the respondents believe that the minority citizens in their jurisdictions think that "'racial profiling/stereotyping' or biased policing" is not a problem, and another one-third (33%) believe minority citizens view it as a minor problem. Only 12 percent report that minority citizens view racial profiling as somewhat or very serious.

There is a positive correlation between department size and perceptions that racial profiling is a problem. That is, respondents from larger departments are more likely to perceive a problem in their jurisdictions than are respondents from smaller agencies.[6] It is important to note, however, that despite this

---

[6] Spearman's rho value = 0.214 ($p > 0.01$)

difference, most of the respondents from larger agencies (e.g., 83.5% of respondents from agencies with 250 or more personnel) believe that racial profiling is not a problem or is only a slight problem. Similarly, respondents from the larger agencies are more likely than their counterparts in smaller agencies to perceive that minority citizens believe racial profiling is a problem.[7] Again, however, most of these large-agency respondents perceive low levels of concern among minority citizens.

We asked the respondents to characterize the "relationship between [their] department and [their] racial minority citizens/community." The vast majority of respondents characterized the relationship as either very positive (32.1%) or somewhat positive (47.4%). Only 1.5 percent characterized the relationship as negative.

A survey item requested that respondents indicate what activities their departments had engaged in as a result of "current events related to 'racial profiling.'" The survey listed six particular activities and allowed departments to list "other" activities. More than half of the responding agencies (56.1%) had engaged in one or more of the listed activities. As indicated in Figure 2, more than one-third of the agencies (37.4%) had held "formal internal discussions of racial profiling or racial stereotyping." Almost one-fifth (18.9%) had adopted new policies, and 12.3 percent had modified existing policies. Similar percentages of agencies reported that they had modified academy or in-service training (17.5%), instituted "data collection on race of citizens stopped" (17.5%), or engaged in "enhanced outreach to the community on issues of race" (17%). A small number of agencies listed "other" activities not included on the survey. Specifically, 21 agencies reported that they had held informal internal discussions, 10 had sent representatives to conferences and/or training, and four had created task forces to address the issue.

---

[7] Spearman's rho value = 0.256 ($p > 0.01$)

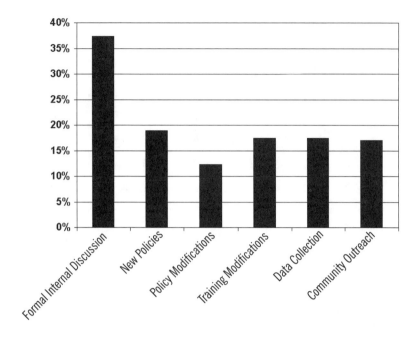

**Fig. 2. Departmental responses to current events related to racial profiling**

As indicated in Figure 3 (see next page), agency responses vary by department size. Specifically, larger departments are more likely than smaller ones to engage in the various activities stimulated by current events related to racial profiling.

The survey helped staff determine what impact public debate and reports of "racial profiling" were having on agencies. Specifically, we asked respondents to indicate how "current events related to 'racial profiling,' including [the] departmental responses to these events," had affected (1) their relationship with minority communities, (2) accusations against their officers of racial profiling and/or biased policing, (3) media coverage of the agency, (4) morale of agency personnel, and (5) activity levels (e.g., number of vehicle stops) of their line personnel. For each question, the respondent designated a number between one and five, with "1" indicating a negative impact, "3" indicating no impact, and "5" indicating a positive impact.

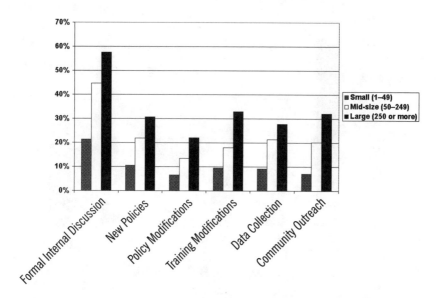

**Fig. 3. Departmental responses by department size (number of officers)**

Overwhelmingly, departments reported no impact across all five areas; specifically, between 72.6 percent and 90.6 percent reported no impact for each of the five items.

Where impact *was* reported, it was more likely to be positive with regard to departments' relationships with minority communities, and more likely to be negative with regard to department morale and accusations against officers. Because of the overwhelming finding of no impact, we did not conduct analyses to assess the relationship between departmental activities (e.g., enhanced outreach to minority communities) and the various impacts (e.g., relationships with minority communities).

An open-ended item asked, "What resources do departments need to help them deal with either the incidence of racially biased policing or the community perception thereof?" Respondents reported that they needed funds for training, education, equipment, and/or technology. Some also indicated that they could better handle the problems if the department and the media had a more positive relationship.

## CONCLUSIONS

Information generated in our citizen focus groups is consistent with national surveys that indicate that many citizens—particularly racial and ethnic minorities—perceive the existence of various forms of racially biased policing, including "racial profiling." Practitioner focus groups and survey responses indicate that law enforcement personnel perceive the problem to be less serious than does the public. These differing perceptions may be partly a function of definitions. As previously discussed, we perceive that citizens and police are defining the problem very differently— with citizens defining the problem very broadly, and many police practitioners defining the problem only as stops based "solely" on race. When we asked citizens and police around the same table specifically about "racially biased policing," perceptions of seriousness started to converge. Further, both groups believed that activities could be implemented to reduce both racially biased policing and the perceptions thereof. Both citizens and practitioners want to prevent the disparate targeting of various racial/ethnic groups and the differential treatment of people with whom police engage.

Of course, we don't know and, in fact, likely can never know exactly how much biased policing there is, and when and where it occurs. Nor can we know the extent to which citizens' *perceptions* of biased policing do, in fact, accurately reflect officer behavior and motivation. However, we do not believe that jurisdictions need the precise answers to these questions before they can act. To the contrary, we believe agency executives should lead their communities in discussions about racially biased policing and the perceptions thereof, and work with citizens to develop responses to both. In the subsequent chapters, we provide recommendations for jurisdictions to consider in the course of this collaborative process.

# Appendix: PERF Survey on Issues Related to "Racial Profiling"

**PERF Survey on Issues Related to "Racial Profiling"**

POLICE EXECUTIVE
RESEARCH FORUM

October 16, 2000

Dear Agency Executive:

PERF is conducting a project related to the very potent topic of "Racial Profiling" with financial support from the Office of Community Oriented Policing Services. As part of that study, we have enclosed a survey that we hope you will complete and return to us.

In this survey, we have broken down the broad (and frequently misused) term "racial profiling" into what we believe are the two key issues facing law enforcement: racially biased policing and citizen *perceptions* that policing is racially biased. We know that many departments are seeking ways to deal with both of these issues. In fact, you'll note that some of the questions in the survey are designed to identify promising practices. With this information, PERF will produce a web-based clearinghouse of effective policies and curricula and develop recommendations that draw upon the best ideas from around the country.

### INSTRUCTIONS

These surveys will be scanned into a computer. To facilitate effective scanning, please:

* Use a blue or black ink pen. (Do not use a pencil or typewriter.)
* Write as neatly as possible withot touching the sides of the text boxes.
* Completely blacken the check boxes (e.g., ■ ).

Please return this survey no later than **October 31, 2000**. Thank you very much for your assistance with this important project. Please feel free to call me or my associate, Bruce Kubu, if you have any questions or comments.

Sincerely,

Lorie A. Fridell, Ph.D.
Director of Research
lfridell@policeforum.org

5721071283

## PERF Survey on Issues Related to "Racial Profiling"

November 7, 2000

Dear Agency Executive:

As mentioned in a previous correspondence, the Police Executive Research Forum (PERF) is conducting a project related to the very important topic of "Racial Profiling" with financial support from the Office of Community Oriented Policing Services. We sent a questionnaire to you on October 16th designed to collect information regarding the issue of racially biased policing and perceptions thereof. If you have already completed this survey, please disregard this letter. If you have not yet completed this survey, we request that you do so by December 1, 2000. Your participation is, of course, voluntary, but would help us to explore this very important topic. **Please respond to this survey even if the issues associated with "Racial Profiling" have not impacted your jurisdiction.** If your agency does not conduct law enforcement activites, please write that on the front of the survey and return it in the self-addressed envelope.

In this survey, we have broken down the broad (and frequently misused) term "racial profiling" into what we believe are the two key issues facing law enforcement: racially biased policing and citizen *perceptions* that policing is racially biased. We know that many departments are seeking ways to deal with both of these issues. In fact, you'll note that some of the questions in the survey are designed to identify promising practices. With this information, PERF will produce a web-based clearinghouse of effective policies and curricula and develop recommendations that draw upon the best ideas from around the country.

### INSTRUCTIONS

These surveys will be scanned into a computer. To facilitate effective scanning, please:
* Use a blue or black ink pen. (Do not use a pencil or typewriter.)
* Print as neatly as possible withot touching the sides of the text boxes.
* Completely blacken the check boxes (e.g., ■ ).

We request that you respond no later than **Friday, December 1, 2000**. Thank you very much for your assistance with this important project. Please feel free to call me or my associate, Bruce Kubu, if you have any questions or comments.

Sincerely,

Lorie A. Fridell, Ph.D.
Director of Research
lfridell@policeforum.org

3001351159

POLICE EXECUTIVE
RESEARCH FORUM

# PERF Survey on Issues Related to "Racial Profiling"

The Police Executive Research Forum (PERF), with funding from the COPS Office (1999-CK-WX-0076), is conducting a project that examines racially biased policing, and the perceptions that policing is racially biased, in order to produce recommendations to help law enforcement departments deal with both issues.

This survey is just one vehicle for collecting information for this project. With it, we want to determine how racially biased policing and perceptions that policing is racially biased have impacted law enforcement agencies nationwide, determine how departments are responding, and collect and disseminate the best ideas developed by departments. Regarding the latter, we request that you send us copies of various types of policies. We understand that this is a somewhat cumbersome request, but hope you will see this as an opportunity to assist in the development of a central clearinghouse of resources for use by all departments nationwide.

Please be assured that your responses will remain entirely confidential. That is, the results will be reported in the aggregate with no department or respondent names associated with responses.

1. Have the current events related to "racial profiling" led directly to any of the following activities in your department? Check all that apply.
   ☐ Formal internal discussions of racial profiling or racial stereotyping.
   ☐ Modifications to academy and/or in-service training.
   ☐ Modifications to existing policies.
   ☐ Development of new policies.
   ☐ Enhanced outreach to the community on issues of race.
   ☐ Data collection on race of citizens stopped.

   ☐ Other1: [                                                                        ]

   ☐ Other2: [                                                                        ]

2. We want to know whether and how current events related to "racial profiling," including *your departmental response to those events* (for instance, those specified in Question #1), have impacted your department. That is, what has been the impact of current events related to "racial profiling," including your departmental responses to those events, on:

   A. The relationship between your department and racial minority communities (circle one answer)?

   | Negative Impact | | No Impact | | Positive Impact |
   |---|---|---|---|---|
   | 1 | 2 | 3 | 4 | 5 |

   B. Accusations against officers of racial stereotyping and/or biased policing (circle one answer)?

   | Decreased | | No Impact | | Increased |
   |---|---|---|---|---|
   | 1 | 2 | 3 | 4 | 5 |

   C. Media coverage of your agency (circle one answer)?

   | More Negative Coverage | | No Change | | More Positive Coverage |
   |---|---|---|---|---|
   | 1 | 2 | 3 | 4 | 5 |

   D. The morale of your personnel (circle one answer)?

   | Negative Impact | | No Impact | | Positive Impact |
   |---|---|---|---|---|
   | 1 | 2 | 3 | 4 | 5 |

   E. Activity on the part of line personnel (e.g., vehicle stops, arrests) (circle one answer)?

   | Decreased | | No Impact | | Increased |
   |---|---|---|---|---|
   | 1 | 2 | 3 | 4 | 5 |

4906145100

POLICE EXECUTIVE
RESEARCH FORUM

# PERF Survey on Issues Related to "Racial Profiling"

3. Does your department have a written policy that specifically addresses racial profiling, stereotyping, or other biases based upon race?
   ☐ Yes.  Please attach a copy of this policy.
   ☐ No.

4. Does your department have a written policy that specifies when race can be used as *one factor* among several to make policing decisions (e.g., such as decisions to stop, question, search)?
   ☐ Yes.  Please attach a copy of this policy (if different from the one identified in Question #3).
   ☐ No.

5. Has your department initiated the collection of new data or the analysis of existing data for the purpose of assessing the race of citizens encountered, stopped and/or arrested?

   Yes.  Please attach a copy of your protocol, policy and/or data collection instrument.

   No.

   ==>Regardless of whether you answered "Yes" or "No", please indicate one or two of the most important reasons why you made this decision regarding the collection of new data or the analysis of existing data.

   Reason 1:

   Reason 2:

6. What resources did you need or would you need for data collection/analysis?

7. Do you know of any academy or in-service training curricula that is particularly effective in addressing the issues of racial stereotyping or bias in law enforcement?
   ☐ Yes.

   Who provides this training?  Please be as specific as possible so we can contact the providers to learn more about their curricula.

   ☐ No.

## PERF Survey on Issues Related to "Racial Profiling"

8. Describe, if applicable, any special department projects or programs that serve to strengthen the department's relationship with ethnic minority communities.

9. Other than the activities encompassed in the questions above, what have you initiated in response to, or in anticipation of, concerns related to racial bias and/or stereotyping?

10. What resources do departments need to help them deal with either the incidence of racially biased policing or the community perception thereof?

11. How would you characterize the current relationship between your department and your racial minority citizens/community? (circle one answer)

| Very Negative | | | | Very Positive |
|---|---|---|---|---|
| 1 | 2 | 3 | 4 | 5 |

12. To what extent do *you think* "racial profiling/stereotyping" or racially biased policing is a problem in your jurisdiction? (circle one answer)

| Not a Problem | | | | Very Serious Problem |
|---|---|---|---|---|
| 1 | 2 | 3 | 4 | 5 |

13. To what extent do the *racial minority citizens in your jurisdiction think* that "racial profiling/stereotyping" or biased policing is a problem in your jurisdiction (circle one answer)?

| Not a Problem | | | | Very Serious Problem |
|---|---|---|---|---|
| 1 | 2 | 3 | 4 | 5 |

Please provide additional comments:

0047145102

POLICE EXECUTIVE
RESEARCH FORUM

# PERF Survey on Issues Related to "Racial Profiling"

**THANK YOU!**

Thank you for taking the time to complete this survey.  Please do the following:

(1)  Provide the information requested below.  We will use this information only if necessary for purposes of calling to clarify information or learn more about one or more of your initiatives. Again, all of your responses will remain confidential.

Contact Person:

Title/Rank

First name

Last name

Phone number            Extension

(2)  Attach if relevant:

■ Department policy prohibiting the use of race as the sole factor in making policing decisions.

■ Department policy that specifies when race can be used as one factor among several to make policing decisions.

■ Data collection/analysis protocol and/or instrument related to documentation of race of citizen.

(3) Please check the appropriate boxes below if you would like PERF to send you (check all that apply):

☐ Sample policies prohibiting racial profiling.

☐ Sample policies indicating when race can be used as one factor to make policing decisions.

☐ Information regarding data collection protocol.

(4) Place this survey and your attached policies in the enclosed self addressed envelope.  If this envelope has been misplaced, mail to:

Bruce Kubu
PERF
1120 Connecticut Avenue, NW, Suite 930
Washington, DC  20036

Please direct any questions or comments to either Lorie Fridell (lfridell@policeforum.org) or Bruce Kubu (bkubu@policeforum.org) at PERF (202-466-7820).

8171145108

# Accountability and Supervision

Police accountability and supervision are important factors in reducing or eliminating bias in policing. A police agency has two effective levels of accountability for operational performance: the chief executive, and the middle managers and supervisors. In this chapter, we discuss their respective responsibilities and propose recommendations for action.

## CHIEF EXECUTIVE RESPONSIBILITIES

The role of leadership is to inspire to higher purpose and to energize the organization toward achieving its goals. The chief executive sets the tone by word and deed, articulating the mission and the style of operation for all to understand. Chiefs must consistently practice the organization's values in their professional and personal behavior. When things go wrong, such as with the highly charged accusation of biased policing, leadership must respond.

The chief establishes operational and administrative priorities and bears primary responsibility for ensuring a positive working relationship with the policing authority, other government agencies and all elements of the community. The chief is responsible for ensuring that the police function lawfully, protecting the rights of all. The chief is also responsible for ensuring that the community's diverse needs and interests are addressed openly and equitably, with respect and dignity for all.

The chief is responsible for shaping and guiding the organizational culture, and for ensuring that the police meet quality standards. Acumen for strategy and timing is critical for an internal climate that welcomes and adapts to change. Quality performance is a constant demand on the chief's time and attention. Managing the public complaint system with fairness and justice is a critical performance indicator, as complaints are integral to quality control and serve as a sensitive barometer of police-citizen relationships. Chiefs' direction of the performance appraisal process is another critical function, as it affects all staff development. In summary, the good management of the organization is in the chief's hands, with responsibility to provide a vision for the future and to organize, direct and control.

## Human Rights

Policing in a democratic society requires that law enforcement personnel be accountable for their actions based on the principles of legality, subsidiarity and proportionality. Legality addresses whether officers have a clear and public legal authority to act. Subsidiarity addresses whether an action is the least intrusive and least damaging to a subject's rights. Proportionality addresses whether an action is excessive or inefficient in dealing with a situation or problem.

The courts have long been regarded as the first bulwark in the protection of citizens' rights. As democratic principles are infused into law enforcement's basic activities, and as we perceive a broader police role, it is reasonable and desirable to conceive of a greater police role as guardians and protectors of democratic rights. In other words, law enforcement should respect the rights of all citizens to be free from unreasonable government intrusion or police action. Certain initiatives are necessary to bring about this transformation.

The first step is to direct an audit of all operational and administrative practices. Self-evaluation against standards is accepted practice in policing, and the standards for a human rights audit are best worked out in collaboration with experts in the field. Vestiges of institutional racism are often found in long-standing practices that have not been challenged for lack of focused review. For instance, officers acculturized to conduct vehicle checks and searches based on inherently racially biased grounds may not at first recognize that they have been operating "out of policy."

The institutional review should entail, for instance, scrutinizing policy, examining the public complaints system and internal disciplinary records for patterns of bias or rights abuses, checking the agency record of civil litigation and criminal charges, conducting surveys of public opinion, and gathering feedback from frontline supervisors.

Awareness of human rights and correction of improper practices are best ensured by integrating policy amendments into the basic and in-service training curriculum, reinforced by frontline supervisors. Training in the powers of arrest, search and seizure, use of force, communication skills, interrogation techniques, exercise of discretion, conflict management, problem-solving, and decision-making is a vehicle for conveying the significance of human rights. Individually and corporately, the police must pursue excellence and uphold professional standards. Chief executives are responsible for ensuring that their officers' conduct complies with and promotes basic human rights.

*Recommendation: The chief executive should direct an audit of the agency mission and value statements, code of ethics and all policies, procedures and practices to ensure they consistently reflect a commitment to integrity, justice, protection of human rights, and unbiased performance of duties. This audit should be embedded in the ongoing professional standards or quality assurance processes in all agencies, regardless of size.*

*We further recommend that the chief executive consider engaging a qualified professional specializing in human rights in creating the standards that will be used for self-evaluation.*

## Organizational Culture
Leadership effectiveness is influenced by organizational culture, a culture shaped by a host of diverse factors, external and internal. The organization reflects the community's customs and conventions, although not all characteristics may be evenly

represented. Internal factors influencing the culture may include the critical events of the past; the impact of leadership, past and present; the existing climate of labor relations; and the history of economic and political support.

Some occupational stress factors of policing are a negative influence on organizational culture, affecting the frontline officer's willingness to learn and to accept change. These stressors range from disappointing experiences with the criminal justice system to the corrosive impact of shift work and excessive overtime on personal health and family life. These factors can affect the attitude the officer brings to engaging with the public.

A culture that values individual differences, rewards good work and promotes respectful interaction among its members is generally indicative of an organization capable of assimilating change. Healthy organizations invariably place a high value on professional competence, with competence defined as extending beyond the technical aspects of the work to encompass individual and institutional integrity.

Leaders' ability to support, encourage and build on the internal culture's positive aspects is critical to the acceptance of progressive policies and control over attitudes and behavior threatening isolation of the police and disengagement from the public. A heavy burden rests with the chief executive's leadership capacity.

*Recommendation: The chief executive should assess the organizational culture—its strengths and vulnerabilities—identifying occupational stress factors for remedial action and reinforcing activities reflecting appreciation for good work, individual differences and respectful interaction among all employees.*

## Quality Assurance

An agency's capacity to change and adjust to a higher level of awareness and compliance with expectations depends on the quality of its operation. The first level of quality assurance with decentralized systems rests with recruitment and selection, addressed elsewhere in this report. The good character and personal integrity of the officer are paramount to ensuring honesty and respectful behavior.

The next most critical element is the means by which the department's values are communicated. Mission and value statements and an aspirational code of ethics are the standards by which the agency and its members are measured.

The third level is quality control. Quality control and organizational integrity are founded on standards, inspection and audit systems. Firm and consistent enforcement of policies and procedures ensures quality results. Lax enforcement opens the door to mediocrity and eventual decline, as well as institutional and individual malfeasance. Supervisors are responsible for ensuring that frontline officers comply with policy. Middle managers are responsible for spot-checking behavior and written reports, and for encouraging and supporting supervisors in maintaining high standards.

Audit and inspection systems provide the structure for institutional overview and quality assurance. There are various local, state and national standards for comprehensive quality control. A well-managed agency will apply these standards, meeting and exceeding them in a process of continuous improvement.

*Recommendation: The chief executive should focus the agency on quality assurance methods in all aspects of operation— directing, supporting and managing internal controls and employing state, local and national standards whenever possible.*

## Diversity

Valuing diversity is a fundamental premise of democratic government. Regrettably, there are times when acceptance of diversity is lost in a well-intentioned zeal for conformity. The police bear responsibility for law enforcement, as well as maintaining peace and order. The good officer continually scans the environment for anomalies to normalcy—for conditions, people and behavior that are unusual for that environment. In learning and practicing their craft, officers quickly develop a sense for what is normal and expected, and conversely, for what is not. The true anomalies offer valuable information on potential threats to people, breaches of the law or disturbances of the peace. No one would expect an officer to fail to act on spotting a weeping child in the custody of someone who did not behave as a parent, or to idly watch a person lurking suspiciously near parked cars.

If an officer is operating on a limited set of expectations of the normal, any manner of characteristics or behavior may engage his or her attention as "anomalies." These characteristics may be style of clothing, differences in gestures or vocal expression, or variation in culture or race. If officers are operating on a narrow set of perceptions, they may draw false conclusions and check people out on grounds that are unwarranted, unreasonable and unsupported by law.

The chief must be acutely aware of the community's social environment and ensure that officers are educated about the community's racial and cultural diversity, and about diversity beyond the local jurisdiction's limits. Policing has approached this challenge in the past through recruit and in-service diversity training, but with uncertain results. In too many instances, frontline officers have concluded that the training was premised on the assumption that all officers are inherently biased and prejudiced. Resentment has often overshadowed good intent. More recently, agencies have found that integrating the theme of racial and cultural diversity into mainstream curriculum subjects, and into normal and everyday functions, is a much more successful approach.

The principle of valuing diversity finds expression in the racial composition of the department, content of the recruit and in-service training curriculum, employment of minority race trainers, provision of educational material, and provision of support in word and deed by leaders at all levels. Participation in training programs by community members and human rights specialists will also help to ensure a culture of openness and external partnerships, if the participation is consistent with training goals. Evaluation of diversity training is accomplished by linking training objectives to operational outcomes.

Respect and appreciation for diversity relating to gender, race, victims, and people with special needs are central to recognizing human rights. Police agencies that understand and value diverse communities create structures and systems that reach outward, enjoining and empowering police officers and citizens to collaborate in problem-solving on issues of crime and disorder.

*Recommendation: The chief executive should assess the need to introduce or reinforce an integrated approach for encouraging police awareness and appreciation of racial/ethnic diversity and cultural differences.*

## Public Complaints

Public complaints have long been regarded as an indicator of the climate existing between the public and frontline officers. The growing number of civilian oversight agencies have sprung from the belief that complaint investigation cannot be left solely to police leadership, and that the public interest is best served by some outside assessment and disposition. While well-intended and, in some cases, contributing positively to the transparency of the process, in general, civilian oversight committees have proven as bureaucratic and uncertain in their results as the internal systems they replaced.[1]

It falls to the chief executive to set the tone, establish the policies, systems and procedures and, in many cases, ultimately decide the merit of public complaints. A record system with a separate category for complaints of biased policing will afford the chief an opportunity to monitor and respond publicly to questions of alleged improper discrimination by race, perceived or well-founded. Above all, the reception system must ensure that complainants are not subject to any form of discouragement, intimidation or coercion.

*Recommendation: The chief executive should direct regular reviews of the complaint reception process to ensure that complainants are not subject to any form of discouragement, intimidation or coercion in filing their complaints.*

*We further recommend that the public complaint management system include a separate category to permit clear and*

---

[1] For more information on citizen review of police, see Walker, S. (1995). *Citizen Review Resource Manual.* Washington, D.C.: Police Executive Research Forum.

*accurate monitoring of complaints of biased policing, with the capacity to identify patterns and practices inimical to equal treatment of citizens.*

## Public Complaint Audits

The chief executive should monitor complaint systems through periodic reviews of the nature and incidence of complaints and spot-checks of individual files. Regular reviews should assess the total number of complaints and complaints broken down by type; by involvement of individual officers, teams of officers or groups of officers; and by geographic district and command. The audit should take into account factors such as chronic complainers, false or frivolous complaints and complaints calculated to deter officers from performing a lawful duty.

The audit may encompass integrity testing, internal records and control assessments, accessibility reviews, timeliness standards, and complaint disposition. Agencies contemplating the introduction of integrity testing will prudently obtain legal advice, review the impact on discipline codes and labor agreements, and consult with union representatives. Spot-checks of completed files are a useful way to assess performance, together with surveys of complainants conducted at regular intervals. Active participation by an external review body may help to ensure the transparency of the process and respect for the public interest.

*Recommendation: The chief executive should provide for regular audits of the complaint system, comparing performance against policy and using spot-checks and reviews to evaluate effectiveness and efficiency.*

## Officer Performance Measures

Annual and periodic performance appraisals offer outstanding opportunities for recognizing good performance and introducing persuasive behavior modification when necessary. The appraisal instrument should provide an opportunity to grade officers on their communication skills, ability to carry out duties absent of bias, and ability to demonstrate tolerance and respect for human rights in enforcing the law. Above all, the appraisal process should ensure opportunities for positive re-inforcement for doing the right things, and doing things right.

Many progressive law enforcement organizations are implementing record systems with decision-prompting mechanisms called "early warning systems." These systems collect occurrence data on a broad selection of individual performance indicators, not only from public complaints, but other elements of an officer's performance from disciplinary actions, vehicle collisions, absenteeism reports, performance appraisals, personal problems, and training results. Any employee activity that could signal the presence of stress, dysfunctional behavior or a training need becomes the subject of record. To provide for balance and equity, data collection could include positive inputs such as commendations, letters of appreciation and awards.

Within the system, there are triggers calling for management review. For example, three public complaints within a prescribed period would call for a supervisory review and personal interview of the subject officer. Depending on the system's design, any combination of events could do the same. On the premise that the totality of behavior may indicate a developing problem, the supervisor has the opportunity to intervene. The more progressive systems are designed to bring about constructive outcomes, providing the ability to select from an array of remedies drawn from employee assistance programs and staffing actions.

Police personnel should understand a number of things about such systems. They should understand whether the systems are based solely on an analysis of citizen complaints, or on a broader analysis of the patterns of individual officers' enforcement decisions and other performance indicators. They should understand who is reviewing the data, and what standards are used to determine whether an officer's activity suggests possible racial bias. They should understand the possible consequences of being identified as a potentially racially biased officer.

*Recommendation: The chief executive should study the advantages offered by early warning systems and consider a design appropriate to the agency's particular conditions and needs.*

## MIDDLE MANAGER AND SUPERVISOR RESPONSIBILITIES

Close supervision over all public contacts is difficult to ensure, and few police organizations today can offer close supervision over all officers' behavior. The tasks of policing are most often performed by a single officer or pairs of officers operating in a detached assignment, without on-site institutional oversight or independent observers.

An increasing number of agencies are pursuing community policing, with its inherent philosophy of decentralization—dismantling the hierarchy and delegating responsibility to frontline officers. This philosophy stresses self-discipline and personal accountability, and supervisors are encouraged to practice their skills in coordination and coaching. Even in the traditional command-and-control systems, supervisory oversight has been curtailed as downsizing and other efficiency measures have decimated middle management and broadened the span of control. These conditions by no means relieve the supervisor of responsibility for control functions; rather, they illustrate the added burden management strategies place on supervisors.

Policing is a round-the-clock function, and in the larger police departments and state police agencies, the posts, divisions and detachments may be widely separated. While top management's influence is always important, it is the frontline supervisor and middle manager who capture frontline officers' attention. Sergeants, lieutenants and captains wield by far the most powerful influence over the day-to-day activity, attitude and behavior of operational police officers. These supervisors must take responsibility for carrying out any effective program of change or reinforcement of behavior. They cannot do this without clarity in their assignments and expectations.

*Recommendation: As a preliminary to focusing an action program on bias-free performance, chief executives must first clarify for middle managers and supervisors the agency expectations regarding their responsibilities. Top leadership must support and encourage middle managers and supervisors by visibly promoting and enforcing high professional standards.*

Leaders at the supervisory level must exercise motivational and control practices that ensure officers are operating within policy at all times, and through word and action represent the agency's ethical commitments. The frontline supervisors and managers have responsibility for reinforcing the organizational culture's positive aspects in public and in the station. Frontline leaders must consistently support and personally demonstrate respect for the rights of all citizens. The responsibility for control and the exercise of discipline when officers disregard standards concerning the treatment of citizens are major obligations.

Supervisors will realize, however, that many police officers in good faith insist that race does not affect their decisions. Indeed, there is evidence that suspects' attitudes and actions determine officers' enforcement decisions. Officers can be encouraged to go beyond this observation to consider how suspects' actions and attitudes toward police might be affected by their own perceptions of racial bias. Officers need not be made to feel that suspects who behave badly to police are blameless in order to acknowledge that there may be room to improve the overall relationship between police and minority citizens.

*Recommendation: Middle managers and supervisors should ensure that all officers under their supervision are familiar with the spirit and intent of policy in dealing professionally, ethically and respectfully with the public, and that officers are complying with orders. This goes hand in hand with respecting officers' perceptions of offenders and encouraging them to gain insights into their own responses.*

## Officer Probation and Mentoring

New officers on probation are impressionable, and their first experiences with senior-officer partners often establish their patterns of behavior. These early opportunities for imprinting merit the highest priority within the organization. Coach or mentoring officers must be carefully selected from among those known to operate within policy and with a record of respectful relations with the public. A probationary officer assessment system should include a category for evaluating the probationer's skills in communicating, manner of dealing with the public, and knowledge of the law relating to protecting human rights.

*Recommendation: Middle managers and firstline supervisors should pay particular attention to the assignment of probationary officers or officers undergoing field training to ensure they are partnered with experienced officers known to operate within policy.*

*We further recommend that the field training reporting system have categories for evaluating skills in communicating, manner of dealing with the public, and knowledge relating to protection of human rights.*

### Spot-Checks and Monitoring

The firstline supervisor has the responsibility to spot-check officer performance in a variety of circumstances, observing the style of verbal communication, use of safety tactics, and quality of discretionary decision-making and enforcement action. In particular, spot-checks should focus on vehicle stops on suspected drug law violations to ensure that officers follow all departmental policies and procedures, and that they do not go beyond the limits of reasonableness. The supervisor establishes the principle of balance and proportionality in the exercise of discretion through monitoring and coaching. Agency activity reports, including all available data on officer-initiated vehicle stops, will be helpful to the supervisor's review.

The supervisor must be alert to any pattern or practice of possible discriminatory treatment by individual officers or squads. Periodic sampling of in-car videotapes, radio transmissions, and in-car computer and central communications records is effective for determining if both formal and informal communications are professional and free from racial bias and other disrespect. The department should inform officers of the monitoring procedure in advance, with periodic reminders. Corrective action, when warranted, should normally be carried out by the frontline supervisor. In some cases, disciplinary action may be warranted. Conversely, officers consistently observed to operate within policy should be favorably recognized through their annual and periodic appraisal reports.

Middle managers and supervisors must be alert to new laws and court decisions affecting critical procedures of arrest, search and seizure, and use of force—informing, monitoring and coaching officers about the impact of updated interpretations of the law. Learning from mistakes and reacting positively to new conditions are simply intelligent approaches to law enforcement. In instructing frontline officers, supervisors must take care to present change in a positive way, and not as a hindrance to obtaining results.

*Recommendation: Supervisors should monitor activity reports for evidence of improper practices and patterns. They should conduct spot-checks and regular sampling of in-car videotapes, radio transmissions, and in-car computer and central communications records to determine if both formal and informal communications are professional and free from racial bias and other disrespect.*

## Public Complaint Processing

The sergeant, lieutenant or captain is often the first point of contact for citizens lodging a complaint at a police station. How complainants are received and addressed makes an indelible impression on his or her sense of trust and confidence in the agency's ability and willingness to accord the complaint a fair hearing. The officer has the responsibility to ensure that complaints are received with formality, that all departmental procedures are carried out to the letter, and that complainants are treated with respect. The ranking police representative should ensure that complainants are not subjected to any form of discouragement, intimidation or coercion.

The complainant's comments should be recorded and provided to the departmental investigation unit. The complainant must be provided with information on how the department deals with complaints, and be given the name of the office responsible for handling them.

*Recommendation: Middle managers and supervisors should accept responsibility for ensuring that citizen complaints of biased policing are given a formal and respectful hearing, and that com-*

*plaints are documented in accordance with agency policy. The rank-ing police representative should ensure that complainants are not subjected to any form of discouragement, intimidation or coercion in filing their complaints at the police station or in bringing their complaints to the attention of any officer.*

*We further recommend that middle managers and supervi-sors provide the complainant with information on how the de-partment deals with complaints, and with the name of the office responsible for handling them.*

# A Policy To Address Racially Biased Policing and the Perceptions Thereof

In Chapter 1, we specified that racially biased policing occurs when law enforcement inappropriately considers race or ethnicity in deciding with whom and how to intervene in an enforcement capacity. In this chapter, we propose a policy for police agency adoption that reflects this definition, addressing both racially biased policing and the perceptions thereof. This policy was based on information collected from the focus groups, the national survey, existing policies, constitutional law scholars, law enforcement agency counsel, and others with expertise. Specifically, the policy we propose

- emphasizes that arrests, traffic stops, investigative detentions, searches, and property seizures must be based on reasonable suspicion or probable cause;[1]
- restricts officers' ability to use race/ethnicity in establishing reasonable suspicion or probable cause

---

[1] This particular provision addresses only those activities that require reasonable suspicion or probable cause. The policy wording reflects the fact that not all detentions (e.g., at sobriety checkpoints) or all searches (e.g., consent searches) require either reasonable suspicion or probable cause. These other activities are not prohibited by the policy.

to those situations in which trustworthy, locally relevant information links a person or persons of a specific race/ethnicity to a particular unlawful incident(s);[2]

- applies the restrictions above to requests for consent searches and even those "nonconsensual encounters" that do not amount to legal detentions;
- articulates that the use of race and ethnicity must be in accordance with the equal protection clause of the 14th Amendment; and
- includes provisions related to officer behavior during encounters that can serve to prevent perceptions of racially biased policing.

*Recommendation: Departments adopt the policy set forth in this chapter.*

## BACKGROUND

PERF's national survey indicates that, as a result of recent high-profile events related to "racial profiling," 12 percent of law enforcement agencies surveyed have modified existing policies, and 19 percent have adopted new policies. PERF asked the respondents to include copies of their policies when they returned their surveys. Staff review of these policies determined that most of them prohibit officers from enforcement action (e.g., stops, arrests and searches) "based solely on an individual's race." While the policies convey the positive message that the police agencies will not tolerate "racial profiling," they do not provide sufficient guidance on the use of race to make law enforcement decisions.[3] Agencies can do more than reiterate what

---

[2] In some situations, the link may be made to civil violations as well as "unlawful incidents."

[3] Note that agencies with this type of provision may very well have additional, broader provisions elsewhere in policy and/or may provide more guidance to their officers in training.

has always been unconstitutional—that police actions cannot be based solely on race.[4]

The policy we propose specifies when it is and is not appropriate to consider race/ethnicity in making law enforcement decisions. This policy defines "racially biased policing" building on Fourth Amendment (Search and Seizure)[5] and 14th Amendment (Equal Protection)[6] principles. The complementary provisions clarify when officers *can* use race/ethnicity as a factor to establish reasonable suspicion or probable cause and provide similar clarity for using race/ethnicity in making other law enforcement decisions. It also includes procedures that can reduce *perceptions* of racially biased policing.

We start by setting forth the policy itself. We then discuss and elaborate on the content.

## THE POLICY

*Title:*     *Addressing Racially Biased Policing and the Perceptions Thereof*

*Purpose:*   *This policy is intended to reaffirm this department's commitment to unbiased policing, to clarify the circumstances in which officers can consider race/ethnicity when making law enforcement decisions, and to reinforce procedures that*

---

[4] For example, in *U.S. v. Brignoni-Ponce*, a Fourth Amendment case regarding a vehicle stop near a border, the Supreme Court held that police cannot stop motorists based solely on their racial or ethnic appearance, even if the officers are investigating illegal aliens (422 U.S. 873, 1975).

[5] "The right of the people to be secure in their persons, houses, papers and effects against unreasonable searches and seizures, shall not be violated; and no warrants shall issue, but upon probable cause, supported by oath or affirmation, and particularly describing the place to be searched, and the persons or things to be seized."

[6] "[N]o State shall make or enforce any law which shall . . . deny to any person within its jurisdiction the equal protection of the laws."

*serve to assure the public that we are providing service and enforcing laws in an equitable way.*

*Policy:*
  A) *Policing Impartially*
     1. *Investigative detentions, traffic stops, arrests, searches, and property seizures by officers will be based on a standard of reasonable suspicion or probable cause in accordance with the Fourth Amendment of the U.S. Constitution. Officers must be able to articulate specific facts and circumstances that support reasonable suspicion or probable cause for investigative detentions, traffic stops, arrests nonconsensual searches, and property seizures.*

       *Except as provided below, officers shall not consider race/ethnicity in establishing either reasonable suspicion or probable cause. Similarly, except as provided below, officers shall not consider race/ethnicity in deciding to initiate even those nonconsensual encounters that do not amount to legal detentions or to request consent to search.*

       *Officers may take into account the reported race or ethnicity of a specific suspect or suspects based on trustworthy, locally relevant information that links a person or persons of a specific race/ethnicity to a particular unlawful incident(s). Race/ethnicity can never be used as the sole basis for probable cause or reasonable suspicion.*
     2. *Except as provided above, race/ethnicity shall not be motivating factors in making law enforcement decisions.*

  B) *Preventing Perceptions of Biased Policing*
    *In an effort to prevent inappropriate perceptions of biased law enforcement, each officer shall do the following when conducting pedestrian and vehicle stops:*

    • *Be courteous and professional.*

- *Introduce him- or herself to the citizen (providing name and agency affiliation), and state the reason for the stop as soon as practical, unless providing this information will compromise officer or public safety. In vehicle stops, the officer shall provide this information before asking the driver for his or her license and registration.*
- *Ensure that the detention is no longer than necessary to take appropriate action for the known or suspected offense, and that the citizen understands the purpose of reasonable delays.*
- *Answer any questions the citizen may have, including explaining options for traffic citation disposition, if relevant.*
- *Provide his or her name and badge number when requested, in writing or on a business card.*
- *Apologize and/or explain if he or she determines that the reasonable suspicion was unfounded (e.g., after an investigatory stop).*

*Compliance:*
*Violations of this policy shall result in disciplinary action as set forth in the department's rules and regulations.*

*Supervision and Accountability:*
*Supervisors shall ensure that all personnel in their command are familiar with the content of this policy and are operating in compliance with it.*

## DISCUSSION

### Title and Purpose
We titled the policy "Addressing Racially Biased Policing and the Perceptions Thereof" to reflect our strong preference for the term "racially biased policing" over "racial profiling," and to reflect the importance of addressing both the instances of and the perceptions of its practice. The policy's stated purpose is "to reaffirm [the] department's commitment to unbiased policing, to clarify the circumstances in which officers can con-

sider race/ethnicity when making law enforcement decisions, and to reinforce procedures that serve to assure the public that [the department is] providing service and enforcing laws in an equitable way." Importantly, while this policy addresses *racially* biased policing, agencies could adapt it to cover biased policing related to gender, age, etc.

## Policing Impartially

*Using Race/Ethnicity as a Factor To Establish Reasonable Suspicion or Probable Cause*

One aspect of ensuring the unbiased treatment of citizens is to consistently apply the standards of reasonable suspicion and probable cause to law enforcement interventions. The proposed policy affirms these Fourth Amendment requirements. Specifically, the policy reads as follows:

> Investigative detentions, traffic stops, arrests, searches, and property seizures by officers will be based on a standard of reasonable suspicion or probable cause in accordance with the Fourth Amendment of the U.S. Constitution. Officers must be able to articulate specific facts and circumstances that support reasonable suspicion or probable cause for investigative detentions, traffic stops, arrests, nonconsensual searches, and property seizures.

However, the policy goes beyond reaffirmation of the constitutional provisions and provides clarity to these standards of proof. Specifically, the policy sets forth limits on when officers can consider race/ethnicity to establish probable cause[7] or

---

[7] Probable cause for a warrant or warrantless arrest exists when "the facts and circumstances within the officers' knowledge and of which they had reasonably trustworthy information are sufficient in themselves to warrant a man of reasonable caution in the belief that an offense has been or is being committed" (*Brinegar v. United States*, 338 U.S. 160, 1949). Probable cause is required for some searches and applies the above requirements (i.e., "facts and circumstances...") to the belief that seizeable evidence is in a particular location.

reasonable suspicion.[8] We identified this need through our focus groups, in which it became very clear that practitioners at all levels—line officers, command staff and executives—have very different perceptions regarding the circumstances in which officers can consider race/ethnicity. Participants discussed when officers can use race/ethnicity as one factor in the "totality of the circumstances" to establish reasonable suspicion or probable cause.[9] We found many differences of opinion among line officers and command staff, even *within* agencies, on this point. Some believed that officers should not use race/ethnicity to justify law enforcement intervention except when specified as part of a suspect's description. Others—when provided with hypothetical examples—clearly revealed an on-the-street use of race/ethnicity as a general indicator of criminal activity.

Our survey data confirm that many agencies do not provide guidance to their line personnel on this point in policy. Just under 4 percent of the responding agencies reported that they have policies that "specify when race can be used as one factor among several to make policing decisions."

While we acknowledge that agencies may, to differing extents, address this issue in training, training alone is not sufficient. Policy is used in policing to provide parameters for officer discretion. Without clear parameters, some officers will, and *do* (as indicated by the focus group data), use race/ethnicity as a general indicator of criminal activity, to help justify, for in-

---

[8] Reasonable suspicion, which is required for detentions, "is a less demanding standard than probable cause...in the sense that reasonable suspicion can be established with information that is different in quantity or content than that required to establish probable cause" (*Alabama v. White*, 496 U.S. 325, 1990).

[9] The Supreme Court has not provided specific guidance in this area; the court's decisions in this realm have addressed only those cases related to illegal aliens (e.g., *United States v. Brignoni-Ponce*, 422 U.S. 873, 1975). In a Ninth Circuit case, it was held that officers could not use race/ethnicity to establish reasonable suspicion in a geographic area where "the majority (or any substantial number) of people" are of that particular race/ethnicity (*United States v. Montero Camargo*, 208 F. 3d 1122, 9th Cir., 2000).

stance, detentions of citizens. *In this environment of minority citizen mistrust of law enforcement, we strongly recommend that agencies set forth written policy parameters on the use of race/ ethnicity to justify law enforcement intervention.* Without clear guidance in *both* policy and training, law enforcement executives risk having line personnel inappropriately intrude on citizens' freedom based on those officers' personal biases as opposed to objective criteria.

The policy we propose prohibits the use of race/ethnicity as a general indicator of criminal activity, but allows officers to consider it in some situations, such as when provided with suspect descriptions. Specifically, the policy states, "Officers may take into account the reported race or ethnicity of a specific suspect or suspects based on trustworthy, locally relevant information that links a person or persons of a specific race/ethnicity to a particular unlawful incident(s). Race can never be used as the sole basis for probable cause or reasonable suspicion."

The standard for "trustworthy" information is the same one that officers should apply to *any* information they use to establish reasonable suspicion or probable cause.[10] It means that the information is worthy of confidence. "Locally relevant" means that the information is relevant to local conditions. In other words, officers cannot rely on widely held stereotypes, or even on the fact that in some areas of the country, a certain race/ ethnicity is linked to a certain crime. Officers have to have information that supports a link between race/ethnicity and a *specific* crime in their *own* jurisdiction.[11] It is not absolutely necessary that the information be *generated* locally, but it is necessary that it be reasonably *relevant* to the local area.[12]

---

[10] For instance, potential sources of trustworthy information include officer observations, tips (e.g., from colleagues or credible witnesses) and crime reports.

[11] This is the case, for instance, when a *local* victim reports that the perpetrator was of a particular race/ethnicity.

[12] This statement recognizes, for instance, the cross-jurisdictional nature of criminal activity. Thus, for instance, if a jurisdiction experienced a great surge in car thefts that were associated with a particular racial/ethnic group, a nearby jurisdiction might reasonably link the crimes to the identified group.

This trustworthy, locally relevant information must *link specific suspected unlawful activity* to a person or persons of a particular race/ethnicity. The requirement of *specific* suspected unlawful activity precludes the use of race/ethnicity as a general indicator of criminal activity. The information must pertain to a specific type of unlawful activity (e.g., a commercial robbery) or category of unlawful activity (e.g., activities related to drug production/distribution). *To allow officers to use race/ ethnicity to establish reasonable suspicion or probable cause based on the fact that most crimes in their jurisdiction are committed by, for instance, Hispanics, would allow officers too much latitude to treat an entire segment of the population as potential suspects and would be prohibited by the policy.*

Below are two examples of situations in which officers, applying the proposed policy, *could* consider race/ethnicity in establishing reasonable suspicion or probable cause:

> Reports of undercover officers and several recent arrests indicate that white students from the local college are buying cocaine at a particular inner-city apartment complex—the residents of which are primarily black. In this situation, applying the proposed policy, an officer could consider the race of citizens visiting this complex as one factor in a set of factors to establish, for instance, reasonable suspicion to detain. (For example, other factors an officer might use when considering the "totality of the circumstances" might include having observed on several subsequent nights a student with prior arrests for drug possession who is evidencing intoxicated behavior going to the residence of a known drug dealer for 2 minutes in the middle of the night.) Thus, the officer could consider race as one factor that could justify a stop that is related to suspicion of drug activity.

> A number of middle school students have reported that Hispanic men are selling guns to stu-

dents in the area immediately surrounding the school. Again, applying the proposed policy, an officer could consider the ethnicity of citizens around the school as one factor in a set of factors to establish, for instance, reasonable suspicion to detain. (For example, the officer might also have obtained corroboration through parents' observations and his or her own observations over several days of a man matching the students' physical description standing in the same location exchanging goods for money with students, as witnesses described.) Thus, the officer could consider ethnicity as one factor in the "totality of the circumstances" that could justify a stop related to suspicion of illegal gun sales.

Below is an example of when the proposed policy would *preclude* the consideration of race/ethnicity:

An officer sees a poorly dressed young African-American male walking in an upper-class white neighborhood. Without trustworthy, locally relevant information linking African-American males to particular crimes in the area, the officer could not consider this person's race as *a factor among others in establishing reasonable suspicion or probable cause.* That is, this policy prohibits officers from detaining people merely because they are purportedly "out of place" by virtue of their race/ethnicity.

*Considering Race/Ethnicity in Initiating Other*
*Nonconsensual Encounters or Requesting Consent To Search*
We have described restrictions on the use of race/ethnicity to justify law enforcement activities that are covered by the Fourth Amendment (e.g., detentions, nonconsensual searches, arrests). Another provision in the policy extends those restrictions to law enforcement activities that fall out-

side Fourth Amendment restrictions, but nonetheless pose great risks of being conducted in a racially/ethnically biased way. Specifically, the policy restricts police consideration of race/ethnicity in decisions to initiate even those nonconsensual encounters that do not amount to detentions,[13] and in decisions to request consent to search. Officers must be able to articulate some reason (not necessarily amounting to reasonable suspicion) for initiating even a nonconsensual encounter that does not amount to a detention or arrest and for requesting consent to search. They cannot justify either action based on race, except when, as previously discussed, they "take into account trustworthy, locally relevant information that links a person or persons of a specific race/ethnicity to a particular unlawful incident(s)."

### Ensuring Equitable Treatment

The policy provisions discussed above do not go far enough to describe and prohibit racially biased policing activities. Although the provisions place restrictions on police using race/ethnicity as information to justify law enforcement interventions, they do not prohibit officers from acting on that information in a biased way, or from otherwise acting in a biased way. That is, those provisions are insufficient alone as they do not prohibit officers from disproportionately targeting certain racial/ethnic groups who are suspected or guilty of breaking the law. Nor do they prohibit officers from otherwise treating people differently (e.g., without dignity and respect) based on race/

---

[13] In other words, this provision extends the restrictions on the use of race/ethnicity to even those nonconsensual encounters that do not require either reasonable suspicion or probable cause. We use the term "nonconsensual encounters" to encompass activities that require reasonable suspicion or probable cause (e.g., arrests, detentions) *as well as* activities that do not require those levels of proof. An example of the latter is when an officer approaches a group of people and asks them who they are and what they are doing. ("Nonconsensual" implies that it is the officer, not the citizens, who initiates the encounter, but it does not *necessarily* imply that the citizens are opposed to the encounter.)

ethnicity. We need the second provision reflecting the general principle of equal protection.

As an example, this second provision prohibits an officer from stopping a white traffic violator and releasing that violator *because* he or she is white, and then stopping a black traffic violator and requesting consent to search *because* that violator is black. Even if the officer has acted in accordance with all Fourth Amendment provisions, he or she has violated the 14th Amendment's Equal Protection clause. As another example, this provision would prohibit officers from conducting *Whren*[14] (that is, "pretext") stops only of a particular racial/ethnic group and not of others, *because* of race/ethnicity. Thus, the policy includes a provision that recommits the department to ensuring equal protection in all aspects of its work: "Except as provided above, race and ethnicity shall not be motivating factors in making law enforcement decisions."

The qualification "except as provided above" is necessary to allow officers, in very restricted circumstances, to treat people differently on the basis of race/ethnicity (for instance, when trustworthy, locally relevant information links a person(s) of a particular race/ethnicity to specific unlawful activity). Those narrow exceptions aside, the provision sets up the "but for" test for officers in evaluating all of their interactions with citizens. For example, officers should ask themselves, "Would I be engaging this person *but for* the fact that this person is black?" "Would I be asking this question of this person *but for* the fact that this person is white?"

Together, the provisions above prohibit racially biased policing. They will prompt officers to carefully consider their motives for engaging citizens, and tightly circumscribe their use of race/ethnicity in making enforcement decisions.

---

[14] In *Whren et al. v. United States* (517 U.S. 806, 1996), the Supreme Court held that, as long as a traffic law is violated, an officer's underlying motive for stopping the vehicle (e.g., to check for drugs) is irrelevant. Important for this discussion, the court noted that conducting selective enforcement on the basis of race (e.g., making a pretext stop *because* of a person's race) is prohibited by the 14th Amendment's Equal Protection clause.

### Preventing Perceptions of Biased Policing

A number of minority citizens who participated in our focus groups acknowledged that they would be much more likely to suspect that a police stop was racially motivated if they were treated discourteously or not informed of the reason rather than being treated with respect and told why the stop was made. Some of the "racial profiling" policies we reviewed reflected this by including provisions emphasizing the need to prevent perceptions of racial bias. Part B of our proposed policy includes some of these directives.

Specifically, we propose that an officer who detains a pedestrian or motorist do the following:[15]

- Be courteous and professional.
- Introduce him- or herself to the citizen (providing name and agency affiliation), and state the reason for the stop as soon as practical, unless providing this information will compromise officer or public safety. In vehicle stops, the officer shall provide this information before asking the driver for his or her license and registration.
- Ensure that the detention is no longer than necessary to take appropriate action for the known or suspected offense, and that the citizen understands the purpose of reasonable delays.
- Answer any questions the citizen may have, including explaining options for traffic citation disposition, if relevant.
- Provide his or her name and badge number when requested, in writing or on a business card.

---

[15] We support, also, the comprehensive list of practices suggested for traffic stops by the National Highway Traffic Safety Administration in its publication, "Strengthening the Citizen and Law Enforcement Partnership at the Traffic Stop: Professionalism Is a Two-Way Street" (DOT HS 809 180, December 2000). See also the relevant provisions in the "Sample Professional Traffic Stops Policy and Procedure" developed by the International Association of Chiefs of Police (n.d.).

- Apologize and/or explain if he or she determines that the reasonable suspicion was unfounded (e.g., after an investigatory stop).

Some of these provisions merit further discussion of how they were developed.

The second provision that directs the officer to introduce him- or herself and provide a reason for the stop was the subject of much focus group discussion. Not surprisingly, virtually all citizens favored initiating stops this way. Practitioners had mixed opinions—some advocated this method of contact, and others criticized it. The critics claimed that they need to get a citizen's license and registration before stating the reason for a stop, lest the citizen argue and refuse to turn over the papers. On the other hand, officers who generally provide the reason for the stop up front said such cases are rare and, when they occur, manageable. We believe that providing an introduction and a reason for a stop sets a professional tenor and establishes clear, direct and respectful communication between the citizen and officer. We believe that these benefits outweigh the infrequent negative citizen response.

Providing a name and badge number upon request is standard within departments, but providing a business card is not. Citizens in our focus groups perceived that action as a very positive sign of professionalism and accountability. Some departments have adopted as standard practice the provision of business cards following all detentions.

Some of the citizens in the focus groups had been detained because, presumably, they resembled someone who was being sought. Many of these participants expressed continued anger over the event, and lamented that "if only" the officer had apologized or explained the circumstances, they would have felt differently. Respectfully explaining a stop and, in some cases, offering an apology for any inconvenience caused by the stop, has great potential for reducing the residual ill effects of such encounters. (The officer is not apologizing for what may have been lawful and proper actions, but rather for the inconvenience and embarrassment the stop caused the citizen.)

## Compliance, Supervision and Accountability

Supervisors have important responsibilities in ensuring compliance with new policies. They must hold those officers who fail to comply accountable, taking disciplinary action as appropriate.

## CONCLUSION

A policy that delimits the circumstances in which race/ethnicity can be considered in law enforcement decisions is critical to any department plan to respond to racially biased policing and the perceptions of its practice. The overwhelming majority of officers on our streets are well-intentioned and do not want to engage in racially biased policing. However, very few departments have meaningful policies that articulate the circumstances in which race/ethnicity can and cannot be used to make decisions. A chief executive must not only declare a prohibition against racially biased policing, but also clearly define the prohibited conduct in policy.

# Recruitment and Hiring

This chapter addresses issues and recommendations related to recruiting and hiring police officers toward the goal of reducing racial bias in policing. While the chapter does not comprehensively cover all issues related to recruitment and hiring of police personnel, it does address those most clearly and directly associated with racial bias. The important, complex legal issues related to affirmative action laws and associated consent decrees are also beyond the scope of this chapter.

Recruitment and hiring policies and practices have the potential to reduce racial bias in policing in two basic ways: (1) by hiring officers who can police in an unbiased manner, and (2) by establishing a police workforce that reflects the racial demographics of the community the agency serves.

## RECRUITING AND HIRING
## UNBIASED POLICE OFFICERS

Good police officers carry out their duties with fairness, integrity, diligence, and impartiality. They respect basic human rights and civil liberties. They know how to communicate effectively and respectfully to people of any race, culture or background. They make the effort to understand the culture, language, mores, and customs of whatever population they are policing, and to get others to understand their own perspective. They look for ways to resolve disputes and address chronic community problems without creating or aggravating racial tension. They do not rely solely on their arrest powers to establish their authority. They exercise their professional discretion thoughtfully and judiciously. They understand why some communities distrust the police as an institution, and work hard to earn their trust. They reject racial and cultural stereotypes, recognizing how unfair, inadequate and even dangerous they are to effective policing. They have the self-confidence and courage that is sometimes needed to reject the biased attitudes and behavior they occasionally find among fellow police officers. These qualities are essential to reducing racial bias in policing.

Many police officers today have these qualities, and it is in no small measure because of how they police that there is not greater tension between the police and citizens in many communities. Police agencies must seek to recruit and hire more applicants who have, and can further develop, these qualities. To recruit and hire such applicants is no simple matter, however. It calls not only for making judgments about applicants' racial attitudes, but also for predicting how applicants would act on those attitudes while working in the highly autonomous and discretionary environment of street policing.

It is important to bear in mind that few, if any, people are totally free of bias in one form or another. Most people stereotype others whom they don't know in some, usually benign, way. The search for unbiased police officers is not a search for the saintly and pure, but rather a search for well-intentioned individuals who, at a minimum, are willing to consider and challenge their own biases and make a conscious effort not to allow them to negatively affect their decision-making as officers. Nor is it the case that racial bias operates only when white police officers are biased against minority citizens. Racial bias in policing can operate in many different directions. Minority officers themselves can harbor biases—against white citizens or members of other minority groups, or even members of their own minority group.

Police recruitment messages should appeal not merely to potential applicants' desire for the adventure of policing or the wages and benefits offered, but also to a spirit of fairness, justice and racial equality. It is important to try to overcome some potential applicants' mistrust of the police institution and the perception that the police serve only to preserve a social order, to the disadvantage of racial and cultural minorities. Recruitment messages should promote policing as an opportunity to serve society in ways that can truly advance justice and racial harmony. These messages might go so far as to acknowledge past problems in policing and the lingering perceptions of racial bias, and to suggest to potential applicants that becoming a police officer is a powerful way to improve conditions. Police executives should solicit input from the community, particularly minority communities, as well as from professional advertisers and marketers in crafting and delivering recruitment messages.

In the search for unbiased police officers, personnel staff must consider applicants' own statements on matters involving race and what background investigations might reveal about applicants' character, reputation and documented history. Applicant interviews, whether conducted by community members or police staff, might include questions that reveal applicants' understanding and attitudes about race relations and police-community relations. Asking the questions alone signals to applicants that their attitudes about race are important to the police agency, and that the agency will not tolerate racial bias. Applicants will sometimes admit to harboring attitudes and opinions that one might expect they would keep to themselves. While not foolproof, if one wants to know about applicants' racial attitudes and biases, there is no better place to start than by asking them directly.

Background investigations should explore many facets of applicants' lives, including clues about how they feel and act toward members of other racial and cultural groups. It is especially important to look for applicants who have some experience interacting with members of other races and cultures, and to assess how well they have done so. While no single factor should dictate whether an agency offers an applicant employment, some factors that personnel staff might consider when assessing an applicant include

- what people of other races and cultures say about the applicant;

- whether the applicant has ever experienced being in the racial minority in any setting; and
- whether the applicant has ever been in a situation where there was racial tension or conflict, and if so, how the applicant handled the situation.

Psychometric instruments have been developed to measure racial attitudes and bias, but few police agencies use them in screening applicants. Perhaps someday such instruments will be validated and gain wider acceptance as a predictive tool for police hiring, but as yet, that has not occurred. Police executives should be open to learning more about using psychometric instruments, but we do not know enough about them to recommend them yet.

*Recommendation: Personnel staff should carefully evaluate applicants' character, reputation and documented history as they relate to racially biased attitudes and behavior.*

## HIRING A RACIALLY DIVERSE POLICE WORKFORCE

A police agency whose officers reflect the racial demographics of the community they serve fulfills several important purposes in reducing racial bias in policing. First, it conveys a sense of equity to the public, especially to minority communities. Second, it increases the probability that, as a whole, the agency will be able to understand the perspectives of its racial minorities and communicate effectively with them. Third, it increases the likelihood that officers will come to better understand and respect various racial and cultural perspectives through their daily interactions with one another.

Agencies' hiring practices are one signal to a community of how police leaders view the relationship of the police with various racial and cultural groups. Diversity in the police ranks is necessary to earn minority trust and manifest equity in the public image of the police. Where the police force reasonably reflects the community's racial makeup, it promotes a general sense of fairness. Where it does not, it invites suspicion and mistrust as to why members of various racial and cultural groups are not willing or able to serve in the police ranks. This is not to say that having a racially representative workforce guarantees that the police agency will be free from racial bias or necessarily perceived as fair by the public, but at a minimum, it can demonstrate a good-faith commitment on the part of police leaders to work toward those goals. Police agencies across America have made substantial progress toward racial representation over the past several decades. Nationally, they have nearly achieved proportional representation of African-American officers.[1] To be sure, this varies across jurisdictions: some police agencies have achieved proportional representation, while others remain far from it. A general sense of fairness in police employment opportunities can reduce underlying mistrust of the police among minority citizens, a mistrust that can affect how minorities and police officers relate to one another on the streets.

Having a racially representative police workforce also enhances the range of experiences and communication skills that are essential to effective policing. Having police officers who understand and empathize with various cultures and socioeconomic conditions can translate into more effective street policing in many ways. In some communities, this means having bilingual officers who can communicate with minorities who don't speak English.

It is well understood that much of racial bias and prejudice stems from people's fear of what (and whom) they do not know. Ignorance of the perspectives, manners and customs of other races and cultures can fuel officers' fears and increases the likelihood that citizens' motives and actions will be misunderstood. It is further well understood that police officers come to form special bonds with and rely heavily on one another. Given the opportunity, they will usually look beyond one another's race and culture to find common bonds and, in the process, almost inevitably come to learn more about, and respect and appreciate, their diverse racial and cultural identities. Simply put, racial bias and prejudice thrive when members of different races are isolated from one another, and they dissipate the more that

---

[1] Reaves, B., and A. Goldberg (1999). *Law Enforcement Management and Administrative Statistics, 1997: Data for Individual State and Local Agencies With 100 or More Officers.* Washington, D.C.: U.S. Department of Justice, Bureau of Justice Statistics.

members of different races interact. Police executives can create such opportunities to interact by surrounding their officers with colleagues of different races and cultures. (Police executives must then, of course, manage their agencies so as not to generate friction and factions along racial lines among the officers, but that discussion goes beyond the scope of this chapter.)

*Recommendation: Police executives should strive to hire a workforce that reflects the highest professional standards and the racial and cultural demographics of the community they serve.*

## RECRUITING MINORITY APPLICANTS

Recruiting minority applicants, especially in highly competitive labor markets, requires commitment and effort. Police executives must communicate that commitment to their recruiting staff and devote the resources necessary to achieve minority recruitment goals.

Police recruiters themselves should reflect the community's racial and cultural makeup. They may well be the only direct contact that potential applicants have with police personnel: meeting officers of different races and cultural backgrounds signals a police agency's interest in recruiting similarly diverse applicants. It is not essential that recruiters always be matched with potential applicants of their own race or culture; at times, though, such matches are helpful. In addition, recruiting materials such as brochures, videos, posters, television commercials, and websites should depict a diverse group of police officers from the agency.

Recruiters must first understand the rationale for hiring a diverse workforce, and be committed to this goal. They must be able to articulate the rationale to potential applicants and to the public at large; they will surely be asked to do so. It is also important that the agency's current employees understand the benefits of a diverse and representative workforce, and that the agency's hiring standards need not and will not be lowered to achieve this objective. Police executives should try to get police union support for minority recruitment. Such efforts help ensure that newly hired minority officers do not enter a hostile organizational environment.

Being committed to a diverse workforce means more than just acknowledging numeric goals. If recruiting and hiring initiatives are to help in reducing racial bias in policing, they must aspire to more than just filling racial quotas. They must strive to bring into the agency people who themselves are committed to policing fairly and without bias.

Recruiters should use several methods for recruiting minority applicants. The particular methods they should adopt will vary from community to community, depending on the available opportunities. Among the many methods for recruiting minority applicants are the following:

- *Recruiting at historically black colleges and universities.* A high percentage of African-American college students are drawn to studies in the social sciences, social work and education, all disciplines that lend themselves well to policing.[2] Historically black colleges and universities, and any college or university with a high minority enrollment, are naturally attractive recruiting grounds for police agencies. Recruiters should introduce themselves to college career counselors and faculty who teach in police-related fields (such as sociology, criminology, criminal justice, and social work), and ask them to be alert for students who show an interest in police work.

- *Recruiting through military channels.* The military forces have succeeded in enlisting large numbers of minorities, and many of them, upon leaving the service, will find another public service such as policing an attractive career. Particularly in times of peace and when military enlistment is strictly voluntary, the military system will have screened, trained and educated many good service personnel who might make similarly good police officers.

---

[2] See, for example, Carter, D., and A. Sapp (1991). *Police Education and Minority Recruitment: The Impact of a College Requirement.* Washington, D.C.: Police Executive Research Forum.

- *Recruiting through current minority police officers.* Most police officers know people who have expressed an interest in joining the police force. Minority officers might know other minorities interested in police work. Recruiters should encourage minority officers to make referrals. Officers who work in high schools should be supplied with recruiting information to cultivate interest in police work among good students, even though most high school graduates will lack the maturity and experience to be hired immediately.

- *Recruiting through the religious community.* Churches, temples, synagogues, and other places of worship are important institutions in many communities, especially in some minority communities. Religious leaders often know people who might be interested in and suited for police work.

- *Recruiting from other fields.* Recruiting efforts should not be limited to searching for young people looking to embark on a first career. Police agencies are increasingly finding excellent older applicants who want to change careers. Social workers, teachers and small-business owners often find policing an attractive second career, and their fields are well represented by minorities in many communities. Some police agencies may do well to reconsider maximum age limits for entry-level positions in order to tap into the second-career labor market.

Some police agencies employ the services of high-profile minorities such as athletes and business executives to promote police work as a career. While this holds some appeal and is unlikely to hurt recruiting efforts, it is likely that most potential applicants are influenced more by people they know and trust than by celebrities.

A final word about recruiting minority applicants: how the police treat minority citizens on the streets can have a profound impact on minority recruitment efforts. Citizens who believe they or someone they know has been treated unfairly by police because of their race will not likely be inclined to consider policing as a career. Not many people join organizations they consider hostile to people like them, even for the purpose of trying to change those organizations. In this respect, it is the patrol officers and detectives who work the streets every day who constitute, for better or worse, the most influential recruiting staff in any police agency.

*Recommendation: Police executives should ensure that special recruiting initiatives designed to attract minority applicants supplement the agency's general recruitment program.*

## MANAGING PERSONNEL SELECTION

Police executives should periodically audit their agency's personnel recruitment and hiring process for two main purposes related to racial bias in policing: (1) to assess to what extent the agency is succeeding in recruiting and hiring applicants, of whatever race or culture, who can police effectively, without racial bias; and (2) to assess whether the process has any adverse impact on the hiring of minority applicants.

The first question to ask is whether, as a general proposition, the process is designed to *screen out* unqualified applicants or to *select in* qualified and desirable applicants. Obviously, all processes do some of both, but the relative emphasis of these two objectives can affect the success of recruitment efforts.

A recruitment and hiring approach that is designed principally to screen out unqualified applicants is reactive. It involves little effort to actively recruit desirable applicants, but rather is restricted to weeding out unwanted applicants and selecting all those who remain. The message conveyed to applicants is that they must prove themselves worthy of joining the agency; this approach entails little effort to sell the agency to desirable applicants. The testing and measuring mechanisms are designed to identify applicants who are demonstrably unqualified. Anyone who exceeds the cutoff scores continues in the process. The agency recruits all applicants in the same way and with the same message, with no special appeal to minority applicants.

By contrast, a recruitment and hiring approach that is designed principally to select in qualified and desirable applicants is proactive. It stresses the positive qualities the agency is looking for, such as sound mind and good character, excellent communication skills, demonstrated public service commitment, problem-solving skills, empathy, and social tolerance. It conveys clear and consistent messages about the value of equitable policing, and that the agency will not tolerate overt racial bias. It tailors recruiting messages to particular target audiences. Once the agency identifies qualified and desirable applicants, it assumes that other employers will seek out those applicants, and so it looks to convince them of the benefits of becoming an officer in that agency. The testing and measuring mechanisms, while also serving to identify patently unqualified applicants, differentiate among qualified applicants to allow recruiters to focus on attracting the best of them. The difference between these recruitment and hiring approaches can spell the difference between succeeding and failing in hiring qualified, unbiased police officers and achieving minority hiring goals, particularly in a highly competitive labor market.

*Recommendation: Personnel selection processes should be geared principally to select in qualified and desirable applicants rather than screen out unqualified applicants.*

Most police personnel selection processes assess applicants along a range of dimensions, including

- basic qualifications such as education, requisite licenses and citizenship;
- intelligence and problem-solving capacity;
- psychological fitness;
- physical fitness and ability;
- current and past illegal drug use;
- character as revealed by criminal record, driving record, work history, military record, credit history, reputation, and sometimes, polygraph examination; and
- racial and cultural biases.

An audit of the personnel selection process should gauge the validity of each job qualification and each testing standard. It should ensure that the job qualifications and testing standards accurately reflect the nature of the police officer's job as the agency expects it to be done. For example, if the agency has embraced the principles and methods of community or problem-oriented policing, the agency, through the personnel selection process, should assess whether applicants have the knowledge, skills and abilities necessary to be effective community or problem-oriented police officers. Job task analyses should be current to validate the selection process.

The audit should also gauge the fairness of each aspect of the selection process and whether the process as a whole, or at any stage, disproportionately disqualifies minority applicants. If there is evidence of disparate impact, the agency should explore the reasons for it and look for ways to remedy it without compromising hiring standards.

Police executives must assess whether the sequence of the various testing stages disproportionately impacts minority applicants. Conventional wisdom suggests that the least expensive tests be conducted first, and the most expensive tests conducted last, to preserve budgetary resources. This is usually a sound recommendation, but if the process as a whole is disproportionately disqualifying minority candidates, some reordering of the sequencing of the stages might prove helpful. For example, if a disproportionate number of minority applicants are failing standard written examinations that measure general knowledge, that testing might be postponed until after personal interviews of applicants have been conducted that might identify those with the character and attitudes the agency desires. Once such an applicant has been identified, both the agency and the applicant might be better motivated to prepare the applicant for the written examination. In many jurisdictions, there are police exam preparatory courses available to applicants. Those applicants who know they stand a good chance of being hired if they pass the written exam might be more motivated to avail themselves of preparatory training and perform better on the written exam. This applies equally to desirable minority and majority applicants.

*Recommendation: Police executives should periodically audit the personnel selection process to ensure that the hiring qualifications and standards are both valid and fair to applicants of all races and cultures.*

In addition to examining the sequencing of the selection process, the audit should assess whether the time between an initial application and a job offer is excessively long, resulting in qualified and desirable applicants' being lost to employers who can hire more expeditiously. Again, the testing standards should not be compromised, nor the process short-circuited, but better management of the process might expedite it.

*Recommendation: Police executives should audit the personnel selection process to ensure that neither the sequencing of the testing stages nor the length of the selection process is hindering minority hiring objectives.*

A special note is in order about whether higher education requirements help or hinder the hiring of minority applicants. Conventional wisdom holds that higher education requirements hinder minority hiring, but past research indicates this is not necessarily so. In some areas of the country, minority applicants tend to be more highly educated than majority applicants.[3] This is especially true in areas where there are plentiful opportunities for minority students to attend college. Given the many benefits police agencies gain from having college-educated officers, notably their greater propensity to relate effectively to people of other races and cultures, higher education requirements need not be sacrificed in the interests of minority recruitment and hiring—they may even advance those interests.

Agencies should also carefully consider the impact of residency requirements on minority recruitment. Many believe that requiring police officers to live in the jurisdictions where they police will work to the advantage of minority applicants. This

---

[3] See Carter and Sapp (1991).

may be true in some, though not all, jurisdictions. Proponents of residency requirements argue that they promote better policing because officers are more likely to know and have a personal stake in a community where they both live and work. This is a difficult proposition to prove or disprove, but residency requirements nearly always have the effect of limiting the potential applicant pool from which police officers will be hired, and that is seldom advantageous in any respect when trying to recruit and hire the best-qualified officers.

With respect to both higher education and residency, it may prove more effective and equitable to advance these worthwhile goals through financial incentives to applicants rather than mandatory requirements. In some jurisdictions, changing education and residency requirements and incentives will require legislation or labor contract negotiations.

*Recommendation: Police executives should consider using financial and other incentives to advance worthwhile higher education and community residency objectives, and in any case, ensure that these objectives do not hinder minority hiring objectives.*

Readers are reminded that the entire personnel selection process is the subject of much legislation and litigation. Large bodies of literature and law guide and govern how any particular police agency should conduct its personnel selection process. Police executives are strongly encouraged to avail themselves of sound and current legal advice when making decisions affecting personnel selection.

*Recommendation: Police executives should avail themselves of sound legal and professional advice when making decisions affecting personnel selection.*

Finally, although this chapter focuses on recruitment and hiring, and not on training (see Chapter 6), an audit of the personnel selection process should extend to looking at whether successful minority applicants are disproportionately dismissed from the agency during subsequent recruit training, field training and probationary employment periods. These stages should properly be viewed as part of the overall personnel selection and development process. Unless and until police officer applicants are serving on the street as permanent officers, their presence in the police organization does little to advance the goal of having a police workforce that reflects community diversity.

*Recommendation: Police executives should determine whether minority recruits are disproportionately dismissed from the agency during recruit training, field training and probationary employment periods, and if so, determine why and seek ways to reduce that disparate impact.*

## CONCLUSION

Recruiting and hiring police officers can help greatly in a comprehensive strategy to reduce racial bias in policing if police executives are firmly committed to employing a qualified and diverse workforce. Hiring standards need not—indeed, *should not*—be lowered as a means to achieve minority hiring objectives. Lowering standards courts disaster for the agency and the community, and is in itself an insidious form of racial bias. There are many capable and conscientious people—of all races and cultures—who would make fine officers and who would police their communities fairly and without racial bias; it is up to police executives and their personnel selection staff to dedicate the effort and resources to find them, hire them and keep them.

# Education and Training VI

## INTRODUCTION

In this chapter, we discuss the role education and training can play in reducing actual and perceived racial bias in policing, and recommend practical steps for police executives to take.[1] We discuss education and training programs specific to the police, as well as programs to educate the public. This is necessarily a broad overview; the particulars of how to implement the recommendations will not be found here. PERF hopes to develop a detailed education and training curriculum in the future. We will provide some additional education and training resources on the portion of our website dedicated to this project (www.policeforum.org) as they become available.

Education and training are but two aspects of what must be a comprehensive strategy. Alone, they will not cure the ills of police racial bias. Policy development, policy enforcement, personnel selection, supervision, community relations, operational strategy, accountability systems, and the tone set by the chief executive must all align toward this goal.

Police executives should be clear about the objectives of various education and training programs presented to police and the community, and understand what such programs can

---

[1] For the purposes of this chapter, "education" is the process of learning cognitively, and "training" is the process of developing skill through repetition.

realistically accomplish. They can convey new information, provide and refine critical skills, encourage compliance with policies and rules, facilitate dialogue, and/or convey a commitment to addressing the problem. They are unlikely, at least in the short term, to alter individuals' fundamental beliefs and biases.

## EDUCATING AND TRAINING POLICE: TOPICS TO ADDRESS

Education and training programs relating to racial bias in policing must be high-quality to be effective. They should be developed with input from police personnel, community members, and professional educators and trainers from outside the agency. Each provides unique skills, perspectives and credibility that, when properly combined, can prove critical to effective learning. Education and training programs relating to racial bias in policing should be carefully monitored and evaluated to ensure they are credible to the participants and cover the issues in sufficient breadth and depth. They should be developed and presented in a genuine spirit of professionalism in which police executives commit themselves to helping their personnel understand and deal more effectively with an extraordinarily complex matter.

Education and training programs to reduce racial bias in policing should not convey an accusatory tone to police personnel. They should engage personnel in discussion, rather than preach to them. They should respect the complexities and subtleties of the problem. Good programs and materials cannot merely be taken off a shelf and presented locally; they should be customized for each agency and community. (Recognizing that many police agencies rely on regional training academies for much of their education and training, we recommend that each agency offer at least *some* agency-specific information to its personnel, covering policies and procedures relating to racial bias, for example, and that conveys leadership's commitment to addressing the problem.)

*Recommendation: Police agencies should develop and deliver education and training programs relating to racial bias in polic-*

*ing as a means to help personnel understand and address a complex issue, without being accusatory.*

*Recommendation: Police and community perspectives must be incorporated in education and training programs relating to racial bias.*
      *We further recommend that education and training programs should be tailored to agency- and community-specific needs, concerns and experiences.*

We do not propose that all of the topics presented here be packaged in a single education and training program. In fact, we do not recommend it. Considerations of racial bias in policing should be woven into many education and training courses, so that police personnel become mindful that all of their actions shape public perceptions of and support for the police. We recognize, of course, that fully integrating discussions of racial bias in policing into other education and training courses takes time, and that it may be necessary to develop a single course of instruction to meet immediate needs.

*Recommendation: Police agencies should integrate education and training relating to racial bias in policing into a wide range of curricula, although a single course of instruction may suit immediate needs.*

The particular topics described below can be addressed in a variety of ways and contexts. They can be tailored for the various police ranks and roles, but all police personnel, including command officers, should participate. Limiting participation to line officers and supervisors invites their resentment and detracts from management's commitment to addressing the issues. Some topics lend themselves to education methods, others to training methods. Some lend themselves to both police and citizen participation; others are better covered with police personnel only. All topics should take into account perspectives from outside the police organization, as well as perspectives unique to the police. What is most important is that the topics and issues be covered openly, honestly and in sufficient depth for real learning to occur.

## Protection of Human and Civil Rights

Discussions of racial bias in policing should begin by having police personnel reflect on the core mission and values of policing. The founding principles of modern policing should be revisited, as should the mission and value statements adopted by the trainees' own agencies. Police personnel should understand that the protection of human and civil rights is a central and affirmative part of the police mission, not an obstacle to effective policing. Among these are the right to equal protection under the law, to be free from unreasonable search and seizure, to be free from compulsory self-incrimination, to have access to counsel, and to be free from unnecessary force and violence. Sacrificing individual rights in the name of law enforcement must be understood as a profound failure of policing, rather than a necessary tradeoff. It is only in this light that apparent conflicts between multiple police objectives can be reconciled.

*Recommendation: All police personnel should receive academy and supplemental recruit training that conveys the message that the protection of human and civil rights is a central part of the police mission, not an obstacle to it.*

## Nature of the Problem

Education and training intended to reduce racial bias in policing should address the nature of the problem. Police personnel need to understand that racial bias is neither a simple nor a one-dimensional issue. It is complex and takes many forms— some obvious, and others subtle. Examples include

- targeting motorists for traffic stops on the basis of racial profiles;
- applying discretionary enforcement on the basis of race;
- tolerating different degrees of disorder and deviance on the basis of race;
- interfering with citizens' routine activities on the basis of race (e.g., stopping, questioning and searching citizens without adequate cause);
- assuming someone is dangerous on the basis of race;

- unduly relying on race as a part of suspect identification; and
- providing different levels of police patrol and protection on the basis of race, or because of unfounded racial fears.

While the vast majority of police officers are not racially biased in either their attitudes or their actions, it cannot be denied that some racial bias *does* exist in policing. It is not solely a matter of individual officers' racist or bigoted views, although that is part of the overall problem. Nor is it solely a matter of officers' intentional misconduct, although that, too, is part of the problem. Racial bias exists in policing because of more complex social and structural reasons, as well, and most police officers recognize this, at least intuitively. Good education and training can help them understand the issues more clearly and allow them to participate in finding solutions to the problem.

*Recommendation: Education and training programs relating to racial bias in policing should more precisely define the numerous dimensions, complexities and subtleties of the problem.*

### Evidence of Racial Bias in Policing

Education and training programs should present what evidence exists about the forms and dimensions of racial bias in policing (see e.g., Walker, Spohn and DeLone 2000; Bureau of Justice Statistics 2001). They should present public opinion and survey data on perceptions of racial bias, as well as statistical data on such things as police stops, searches and arrests, and case dispositions for minority and majority citizens.

Some police officers remain unconvinced of police racial bias, at least in their own agencies. Consequently, evidence for it at the national or state level takes the discussion only so far. For education and training to be most productive, facts from the local level should be presented, as the experiences of police trainees' own agencies and communities are the most relevant to them. Good data may not have been effectively collected or analyzed at the local level, but even in its absence, local experiences should be discussed and considered against the national, state or regional picture.

Racial bias in policing does not manifest itself the same way in every jurisdiction. Thus, it might make sense in one jurisdiction to explore how racial bias plays out in police efforts to interdict illegal drug shipments along major highways, but not make sense to do so in a jurisdiction where drug trafficking is not a major concern. In some jurisdictions, the potential for racially biased policing might manifest itself most prominently in how police handle problems associated with disorderly youth, gangs, migrant workers, or any number of other concerns.

Discussions of the evidence of racial bias need not be limited to the police function, but might profitably extend to the prosecutorial, judicial and correctional functions, as well. This can help police personnel put the issue into a larger context. Well-conducted research, properly presented, can put some facts on the table, facts that can serve as the basis for subsequent discussions about the reasons for racial bias, and what might be done to reduce it.

*Recommendation: Education and training programs should present the available data about racial bias in policing and throughout the criminal justice system.*

### Effects of Racially Biased Policing on
### Individual Citizens, Police and the Community

Surveys indicate that a significant number of minority citizens harbor deep mistrust of the police. Even many white citizens believe that police engage in racial profiling of minorities. Police personnel should consider how the level of public trust in the police affects their ability to carry out their duties. Specifically, they should consider how public support for police policies and initiatives is eroded, how the flow of information from citizens to police so necessary for effective criminal investigations and problem-solving is inhibited, and how police officers themselves are placed at greater risk because of mistrustful citizens who might harm or fail to assist them.

Personal testimonials from minorities who have suffered from the effects of racial profiling or other forms of racial bias in policing can be effective in personalizing the problem and emphasizing the real harm caused to real people. Police personnel need to hear how racially biased actions can have profoundly damaging and long-lasting effects on citizens. Those effects range from embarrassment and humiliation, to fear and mistrust, to anger and rage. For personal testimonials to be most effective, the citizens who talk about their experiences should be credible to the police; there should be no doubt that the poor treatment they received was unwarranted. Known criminal offenders or people who are perceived to be advancing a political cause—while they might have valuable things to say—are unlikely to have the credibility needed to make this method of instruction effective.

*Recommendation: Education and training programs relating to racial bias in policing should convey the impact the problem has on individual citizens, police and the community as a whole.*

## Reasons for Racial Bias in Policing

Having established the nature of the problem and its impact on individuals, police and the community, education and training programs should turn to exploring the reasons for racial bias in policing.

### Racial Bias at the Individual Level

Discussions of the reasons for racial bias in policing commonly start with the biases and prejudices of individual police officers. In many cultural diversity training programs, police personnel are asked to reflect on and discuss their personal biases and prejudices. They are often asked to cite common stereotypes of various racial and ethnic groups, and to test those stereotypes against facts and others' perceptions. Soul-searching exercises such as these may prove useful for some participants, but too often, they also evoke a negative reaction from others. Some police officers might be offended by implications that they are biased, prejudiced or bigoted, and might consequently tune out further discussion of how racial bias in policing can be reduced. If self-assessments of bias are used, trainers should be alert to negative reactions. We are not convinced that, on the whole, having officers discuss their individual biases is the most productive way to work toward reducing racial bias in policing. As we said earlier, it is too much to expect that education and training programs—especially in the short term—will alter individuals' deeply held attitudes and beliefs. Truly biased, prejudiced or bigoted police officers should be identified and dealt with through supervisory and disciplinary processes, rather than through education and training.

Whether or not education and training programs should address racial bias at the individual level is an issue regarding which we make no definitive recommendation. However, we *do* believe that focusing on racial bias at the organizational, institutional and social levels will ultimately prove more productive. Moreover, we believe it is more productive for education and training programs to focus on racially biased *behavior* of police, rather than racially biased *attitudes*.

*Racial Bias at the Organizational, Institutional and Social Levels*
There is ample historical evidence of poor police-minority relations in many places, and even of institutionalized racial bias in some places, during certain periods of time. Today's police personnel should not be made to feel personally responsible for this, but they need to know about it and recognize that larger societal forces—beyond those of individual police officers—have been responsible for some degree of racial bias in policing.

While most of today's police agencies do not engage in the overtly biased actions of yesteryear, other forms of racial bias still present in society can contribute to racial bias in policing, however inadvertently. For example, most of America's communities remain heavily racially segregated, not by law, but often by economic and social forces. Where there is racial bias in bank lending and real-estate marketing practices, there is racial segregation. Heavily segregated communities contribute to police officers' notions of who belongs where, and accordingly, who is suspicious by virtue of their race and where they are. In some communities, for example, blacks are thought not to belong in predominantly white neighborhoods, and vice versa, or Latinos are thought not to belong in Anglo neighborhoods, unless they are there to work. Thus individuals can come under suspicion, largely because it is perceived that they have few legitimate reasons to be out of their "own" neighborhoods. Police commanders may feel pressure, explicit or implicit, to keep those who "do not belong" out of others' neighborhoods.[2] That pressure can easily be passed along to line-level officers, with the expectation that they keep a close watch on individuals who are "out of place." Education and training programs should help police recognize and resist such pressure.

In addition, there are organizational pressures on the police that contribute to racial bias, or perceptions of bias, in policing. In some agencies, police officers are still held to enforcement quotas, whether officially or unofficially. Some newer officers, eager to establish a reputation as being "active," see high-volume enforcement activity as the path to career advancement. Organizational pressures can lead some officers to conclude that conducting a lot of stops and searches will yield a lot of arrests and contraband seizures. Some will go on to conclude that they have a better chance of getting the results they want if they stop and search minorities, a conclusion not supported by the evidence (Harris 1999b; Bureau of Justice Statistics 2001). For officers assigned to special enforcement units, particularly those that emphasize arrests and seizures for drugs and guns, the pressure can be acute. It is helpful for police to recognize and try to address these organizational pressures. Police executives and field commanders must make sure that crime control strategies are consistent with the principles of democratic policing.

One approach to addressing how police should respond to social and institutional pressures that can lead to racial bias in policing is to have officers carefully consider the costs and benefits of being *right* about race-based suspicions, and of being *wrong*. Police are conventionally trained to give more weight to the costs of *not* taking action and being *wrong* (e.g., not stopping a suspicious person who turns out to commit, or to have

---

[2] In fact, in many communities, it is not uncommon for citizens to call the police about a "suspicious" person, a person who is suspicious only for being a minority in a majority area. Such calls put an officer in the untenable position of being asked to respond to a citizen's profiling.

committed, a crime) than to the costs of *taking* action and being wrong (e.g., stopping and frisking a suspicious person who
turns out to be innocent of any wrongdoing). The matrix below
provides a framework for more fully understanding the consequences of race-based policing.

| | Police Take Action on Basis of Race | Police Take No Action |
|---|---|---|
| Criminal Activity Is Occurring, or Has Occurred | "Correct"[3] | "Incorrect" |
| Criminal Activity Is Not Occurring | "Incorrect" | "Correct" |

The following example illustrates what can happen when
police officers use a person's race to make enforcement decisions. Police receive a report of an armed robbery that just occurred in a predominantly white neighborhood. The suspect is
described *only* as a black man. Officers spot a black man in the
vicinity just after the crime has occurred. There are four possible outcomes to the officers' enforcement decisions. Each
outcome has consequences for crime control, individual rights
and public perceptions of the police:

> **Police Take Action on Basis of Race and Crimi-
> nal Activity is Occuring:** The officers decide to
> stop, search and arrest the man based on the
> description of the suspect's race and the man's
> presence in the vicinity. Evidence subsequently
> develops that proves he *is* the correct suspect.
> In this outcome, crime control interests are
> served, even though the officers may have vio-
> lated the man's right to be free from unreason-
> able search and seizure (without a more specific
> suspect description, the police may have lacked

---

[3] Importantly, in using the terms "correct" and "incorrect," we are not judging
the reasonableness of decisions. We use these terms to denote whether the
police action or inaction corresponds to the occurrence or nonoccurrence of
a crime—based on knowledge we would not likely have, but for the fact that
we are dealing in "hypotheticals."

reasonable suspicion to stop him). Public perceptions of the police will likely be mixed; however, because the police got the right man, most of the public will likely support their actions.

**Police Take Action on Basis of Race and Criminal Activity is Not Occuring:** The officers decide to stop and search the man. Subsequent investigation proves he is *not* the correct suspect. In this outcome, there is no impact on crime control, and the officers may have violated the man's rights. As to public perceptions, the police will likely be criticized both for failing to apprehend the correct suspect and for improperly detaining the wrong suspect.

**Police Do Not Take Action on Basis of Race and Criminal Activity is Occuring:** The officers decide not to stop the man (who *is*, in fact, the correct suspect), despite his matching the racial description of the suspect. The officers feel they need a more precise description of the suspect to justify a stop. In this outcome, crime control has been compromised because the offender remains at large. The man's rights have been protected, however. Public perceptions of the police will likely suffer, because they have failed to apprehend the offender.

**Police Do Not Take Action on Basis of Race and Criminal Activity is Not Occuring:** The officers decide not to stop the man (who is *not*, in fact, the correct suspect) because they lack a more precise description of the suspect. In this outcome, there is no impact on crime control, and the man's rights have been protected. Public perceptions of the police will likely be mixed—some people will want the police to be more aggressive in stopping people who even remotely match

the suspect description, while others will feel
the police have used appropriate restraint.

Finally, education and training programs should explore possible perceptions of racial bias as it relates to the operation of the
police agency itself. If there is racial mistrust and tension *among*
police personnel, it is highly likely that some of that mistrust and
tension will show in their attitudes and conduct toward the public. For instance, if racial bias is tolerated within the agency, some
officers might conclude it will be tolerated in police-citizen interactions, as well. Alternatively, officers who feel aggrieved by racial bias within the agency might take out their frustrations on
citizens. These outcomes are not inevitable, but a climate of racial mistrust and tension within the agency, at a minimum, inhib-
its efforts to discuss and address racial bias outside of it. Education
and training programs should address these issues with the ut-
most of care. Feelings may run high, and there may be pending
employee grievances or lawsuits to complicate matters. However,
the sensitivity of the issue and possible legal complexities should
not deter police management from, at a minimum, acknowledging the issue and stating a commitment to working through it
openly and productively.

*Recommendation: Education and training programs relating to*
*racial bias in policing should explore the reasons it exists, espe-*
*cially at the institutional, organizational and social levels.*

### Key Decision Points at Which Racial Bias in Policing Can Occur

As mentioned earlier, racial bias in policing can take a number
of forms. The focus is usually on enforcement decisions officers make at the incident level, namely, on decisions to watch,
stop, search, and arrest suspects. But it is equally, or even more,
crucial for education and training programs to explore racial
bias at the strategic or policy level.

*Enforcement Decisions at the Incident Level*
At the incident level, racial bias can play a part at several key
decision points for police officers, including

- deciding who is worth surveilling for criminal activity—who is worth paying close attention to (including which vehicle tags to run);
- deciding whom to contact or detain to investigate suspicions;
- deciding what attitude to adopt during contacts and stops (e.g., firm, friendly, confrontational);
- deciding what actions to make suspects take during stops (e.g., getting out of vehicles, emptying pockets, keeping hands in sight, assuming a prone position);
- deciding whether and how to explain to citizens the reasons for contacts or stops;
- deciding how long a stop will last (e.g., how long to wait for records checks or canine units for searches);
- deciding whether to search, or request consent to search, people and vehicles, and how extensive and intrusive the search will be;
- deciding how dangerous suspects are, and what level of force (if any) is necessary to control them;
- deciding what enforcement action to take (e.g., no action, verbal warning, citation or summons, custodial arrest); and
- deciding what charges to file (e.g., statutes vs. ordinances, single vs. multiple charges, felonies vs. misdemeanors).

Police personnel should consider what factors they rely on to make such decisions, and how suspects' race may or may not affect their decisions. Many police officers insist, in good faith, that race does not affect their decisions. Indeed, there is evidence to support police claims that suspects' actions and attitudes are the principal influences on officers' enforcement decisions.[4] But

---

[4] See Geller, W., and M. Scott (1992), *Deadly Force: What We Know—A Practitioner's Desk Reference on Police-Involved Shootings*, Washington, D.C.: Police Executive Research Forum, pp. 200–219, for a discussion of research findings related to racial bias in police arrest and use-of-force decisions. Also see Alpert and Dunham (1997), *Force Factor: Measuring Police Use of Force Relative to Suspect Resistance*, Washington, D.C.: Police Executive Research Forum.

police personnel can be encouraged to go beyond this observation to consider how suspects' actions and attitudes toward police might be affected by suspects' general perceptions of police racial bias, and by officers' attitudes and behavior during an encounter. There may be room to improve the overall relationship between police and minorities—even offenders and those who are predisposed to dislike the police—in order to minimize perceptions of racial bias and, consequently, the potential for conflict during contacts, stops and arrests.

*Recommendation: Education and training programs relating to racial bias in policing should identify the key decision points at which racial bias can take effect, at the incident level.*

Education and training programs should cover relevant laws and agency policies that guide and constrain police enforcement decisions where racial bias might come into play. This might include reviews, clarification and discussion of

- statutes and case law relating to search and seizure, custodial interrogation, right to counsel, due process, and equal protection;
- laws and policies that specifically address how officers may and may not use race as a factor in enforcement decisions (see Chapter 4 for the proposed PERF policy on this issue);
- departmental policies governing police discretion, and the factors officers may and may not take into account in the exercise thereof;
- laws and departmental policies relating to so-called "pretext stops," including whether policies are more restrictive than case law, and whether police management encourages or discourages such stops; and
- departmental policies governing how officers should address various types of incidents (e.g., drug offenses, domestic violence and incidents involving people with mental illnesses).

*Enforcement Decisions at the Strategic Level*

It is critical that education and training programs go beyond merely looking at how police officers handle incidents to consider how operational strategy can contribute to racially biased policing and the perceptions thereof. This issue is especially important to police executives, commanders and supervisors—those who make most decisions about which operational strategies to adopt.

The discussion of how police operational strategy might contribute to racial bias in policing should begin by having police personnel challenge some of the assumptions underlying conventional police strategy, which emphasizes criminal and traffic enforcement as the primary means to control crime and disorder. The expectation with the conventional strategy is that numerous stops, searches, citations, and arrests will yield reductions in crime, disorder and accidents. Under certain conditions, and with adequate community input and support, intensive criminal and traffic enforcement may be justified and sensible. But oftentimes, intensive criminal and traffic enforcement falls short of the desired effects, and instead, only worsens the relationship between police and the minority community.

Police personnel should recognize that proactive enforcement strategies should be based on sound research, have the support of the community, and ensure effective crime control while maintaining democratic policing. Police personnel should also be informed about what the research reveals about using race to predict criminality. Many studies have demonstrated that race is not a useful predictor of criminality, either as a sole factor or in combination with other factors.[5] When police use race to predict criminality, their predictions are no more accurate than could be expected if, for example, they stopped people randomly. Police personnel should understand that not only are there legal and moral concerns about targeting minorities for suspicion of criminality, but also that doing so is not an effective crime control strategy. Furthermore, false predictions erode public trust in and support for the police.

---

[5] See Randall Kennedy (1997), *Race, Crime and the Law,* New York: Pantheon Books, chap. 4.

*Recommendation: Police should review how operational strategy can contribute to racially biased policing and the perception thereof.*

### Steps to Reducing Misunderstanding, Conflict and Complaints Due to Perceived Racial Bias

Education and training programs should next turn to ways to minimize the likelihood that valid police actions will be perceived as racially biased.

*Improving Officers' Abilities to Articulate Reasonable Suspicion and Probable Cause*

Police officers should be well trained to articulate, verbally and in writing, what specific information they relied on to establish reasonable suspicion and probable cause. There are usually multiple facts and conclusions that contribute to assessments of reasonable suspicion and probable cause, but some police officers do not know how to properly articulate them. When an officer cannot articulate specific facts and conclusions, prosecutors, defense attorneys and judges are left to speculate as to what the officer was thinking, leaving room for them to conclude that the officer used improper factors such as racial bias in making his or her decisions.

For example, an officer with poor skills in articulating reasonable suspicion might say only that the presence of a Hispanic man in a predominantly white neighborhood led him to suspect criminal activity. The officer might fail to articulate more specific conclusions about the man's behavior, appearance or attitude—conclusions that contributed to the officer's belief that he was engaged in criminal activity. Good skills in differentiating lawful from unlawful conduct must precede skills in articulating suspicions; it may also be the case that teaching officers good skills in articulating suspicions can help improve their skills in differentiating lawful from unlawful conduct.

*Developing Officers' Skills in Handling Conflict*

Police officers should be properly trained to deal with people, including suspects, in ways that minimize the likelihood for misunderstanding, conflict, hostility, and violence. Many police agencies have found training in what is known as "tactical communication" or "verbal judo" to be valuable. Training of this sort should emphasize the importance of providing citizens with adequate explanations for why they have been stopped. Depending on the circumstances, officers can explain their actions either when they initiate the stop or after the stop has been concluded (see Chapter 4 for policy recommendations on this point). Training should also emphasize the benefits of an apology, or at least an adequate explanation, offered to those citizens stopped who prove to be innocent of any wrongdoing. An apology does not suggest that a police officer was wrong for making a stop, but merely that the officer regrets the inconvenience and possible embarrassment caused to the citizen.

*Recommendation: Education and training programs relating to racial bias in policing should teach police ways to reduce misunderstanding, conflict and complaints due to perceived racial bias.*

### Alternative Operational Strategies Less Likely To Be Racially Biased: Community and Problem-Oriented Policing

It is not enough to show police personnel how conventional police strategies can be racially biased. They must be educated and trained in effective alternative strategies that are less racially biased than conventional ones. Community and problem-oriented policing strategies hold just such potential.

Several principles of community and problem-oriented policing are directly relevant to racial bias in policing. Among them is the emphasis placed on having police personnel develop a comprehensive knowledge of the area of the jurisdiction to which they are assigned—whether a beat, a sector or a district. Essential to this understanding is getting to know not only the general demographics of the area—including what *type* of people belong where, and when—but also, to the extent possible, getting to know the particular routines in an area, including which *individuals* normally belong where, and when. For example, knowing that the Hispanic man coming out of the back door of a business in a predominantly black neighborhood after closing time is the owner can prevent a misunderstanding, or worse.

Knowing many citizens by face and name improves officers' abilities to differentiate between suspicious and nonsuspicious people on a basis other than race. Getting to know the community's law-abiding citizens helps police overcome stereotypes based on characteristics such as race. For example, the more young black males officers know by face and name, the less likely they will be to view all young black males as suspects or potential threats.

Actively soliciting community input about crime and disorder problems, what priority each should have, and how they might best be addressed can reveal racial biases that police alone might not recognize. Educating the public about problems can help police secure support and resources for addressing them. Garnering community support, especially minority community support, for police actions can go a long way toward reducing perceptions of racial bias.

Breaking down the broad category of crime and disorder into specific problems, and carefully analyzing those problems, helps police avoid making such crude classifications as "good guys vs. bad guys" and "good neighborhoods vs. bad neighborhoods." It helps police get beyond assumptions about the nature of problems and how to resolve them. Tailoring police and community responses to specific problems on the basis of careful analysis gives decision-makers a better opportunity to consider how various responses might be racially biased *before* those responses occur.

Tactics in addition to, or other than, criminal law enforcement might prove not only more effective in resolving problems, but also less likely to contribute to racial animosity between police and the community. This is especially important in the context of some drug and gang problems, when police enforcement strategies can disproportionately affect young African-American and Latino males (See e.g. Walker, Spohn and DeLone 2000; Walker and Myers 2000). Taking careful measures of the impact responses have on community problems, including the impact on the police-community relationship, can help police refine their responses appropriately.

Educating and training police personnel in community and problem-oriented policing strategies does not guarantee that the strategies will be implemented or that, if they *are* implemented, racial bias will be eliminated from policing. But these strategies, where implemented with the full support of police management, can foster mutual trust and respect between police and communities, and can bring into the open the many aspects of policing where racial bias can play a part.

*Recommendation: Education and training programs relating to racial bias in policing should present alternative operational strategies, in particular, community and problem-oriented policing strategies.*

## EDUCATING CITIZENS

Much can be gained by educating citizens about racial bias in policing, and the perceptions thereof. Many of the issues pertinent to police personnel are also pertinent to the public. As a first step in any citizen education initiative, police leaders should publicly acknowledge the potential for racial bias in policing, and stress their agency's commitment to reducing it. The challenges police face in carrying out their duties should also be addressed: in particular, how public pressure for aggressive law enforcement can contribute to racial bias in policing.

Education programs and materials should inform citizens of what they are obliged to do upon lawful police request. They might also instruct citizens about the proper way to conduct themselves when detained by the police, so as to reduce the likelihood that officers might misunderstand their actions and fear for their own safety. Whereas police personnel are familiar with the requirements of the law relating to stops and searches, some citizens might not be. Police should assure the public that quality policing does not require that constitutional rights be sacrificed in the interests of public order. Finally, education programs and materials should emphasize the need for positive police-community interactions, and encourage citizens to work with the police toward common goals.

Education programs and materials can be tailored for the general public, community leaders, people detained by police, and those who file complaints alleging they have been victims of racially biased policing. Materials and information can be disseminated through the mass media, community meetings, citizen police academies, and personal contacts between police and citizens. In Chapter 7, we discuss how police agencies can more fully engage their communities in discussions about racially biased policing, and work with them to develop effective responses.

*Recommendations: Police executives should publicly acknowledge that the potential for racial bias exists in policing, and commit themselves to reducing that potential.*

*We further recommend police agencies should inform the public about their responsibilities and rights during an encounter with the police. They should reinforce the idea that effective crime control strategies need to be compatible with the protection of human rights and civil liberties.*

# Minority Community Outreach

## INTRODUCTION

Trust is vital to the success of policing in a democratic society, and community outreach is essential for gaining trust. Gaining the trust of minority groups is particularly challenging in light of the long history of strained, and sometimes volatile, relationships between the police and minorities. However, doing so is critically important in the wake of nationwide concern about "racial profiling." Both the incidents and the perceptions of racially biased policing lead to mistrust of the police. Relying as they do on resident input, support and compliance, the police cannot function effectively in communities where tensions are prevalent. Outreach to minority communities is an important component of any departmental strategy to respond to racially biased policing and the perceptions thereof.

Approximately a third of the police departments responding to the PERF survey reported that they have projects or programs to strengthen their relationships with minority communities. While many of these programs focus only on addressing minorities' perceptions of the police, others represent concerted efforts to engage minorities in dialogue and decisions about department operations. The latter types of programs provide the key to developing a respectful and trusting relationship between the police and minorities, and to developing police policies and practices that are not racially biased.

Trust between the police and the community is built through long-term engagement. The police gain respect by consistently demonstrating respect for citizens. Giving up absolute control and allowing citizens to participate in decision-making affecting how they are policed ensures a shared responsibility between the police and the community. Police department efforts to provide significant means for community input into police operational and policy decisions are the backbone of community engagement.

In this chapter, we discuss the importance of effective agency outreach to minority groups, identifying the competencies required. We discuss ways for departments to reach out to minority communities to address racially biased policing, and ways to build and sustain, at a more general level, mutually respectful and trusting relationships. We also describe innovative agency outreach initiatives from around the country.

## NECESSARY POLICE COMPETENCIES FOR MINORITY COMMUNITY OUTREACH

Below we list the competencies necessary for the police to effectively interact with minority groups. Some items apply to all department personnel (including administrative, records and communications staff); others, primarily to line staff and commanders:

- the ability to communicate with residents in their primary language;
- an understanding of cultural issues relating to policing and public safety;
- a respectful approach to relationships with residents;
- the ability to be fair and provide equal treatment;
- the willingness to examine assumptions about links between race/ethnicity and crime in the jurisdiction, in order to bring stereotypes to light;
- interpersonal skills and a sincere interest in engaging with the community;
- the willingness to focus community outreach activities on traditionally underserved populations; and

- a departmental approach to human resources that conveys the same respect for diversity that the department is trying to convey to the community at large.

These foundational competencies are necessary for successful community outreach. Outreach efforts that occur in the absence of these competencies are likely to fail and/or generate cynicism.

*Recommendation: Police department personnel should strive to achieve competence in the areas listed above.*

## EFFECTIVE WAYS FOR MINORITY COMMUNITIES TO GET INVOLVED WITH THE POLICE

Relationships are "two-way streets," and for police-minority relationships to work, minority groups must do more than just verbalize concerns. Minority community members can get involved by

- engaging in dialogue about solutions, rather than about blame;
- encouraging one another to apply for employment with the police department, and supporting those who do through the process;
- developing a broad understanding of professional police practices (perhaps through contacts with national and state police organizations), in order to form an objective standard by which to judge police actions; and
- acknowledging police officers who promote positive police-community relationships with awards or other commendations.

## POLICE ACTIONS THAT HARM RELATIONSHIPS WITH MINORITY GROUPS

Below we list some actions to avoid if a police agency is to maintain successful relationships with minority groups:

- lecturing (educating, without a willingness to be educated);
- withholding information rather than being candid about, and taking responsibility for, incidents that cause harm; and
- becoming defensive (e.g., immediately justifying a deadly use-of-force incident that draws community ire by explaining police policies and procedures, without acknowledging the unfortunate loss of life).

## COMMUNITY ENGAGEMENT ON THE TOPIC OF RACIALLY BIASED POLICING

Police executives should be willing to discuss racially biased policing and the perceptions thereof within their jurisdictions. We believe that constructive dialogue between the police and citizens can lead to an agreement that racially biased policing likely occurs to some unknown degree within the jurisdiction, but perceptions may not always reflect the scope and nature of the problem. With this understanding in place, police and citizens can begin to collaborate to develop ways to address the issues.

## TASK FORCES

A theme throughout this report is that law enforcement should collaborate with citizens. The process of developing remedies in concert with concerned citizens is as important as the remedies themselves. The collaborative process fosters citizens' trust in the police, brings a fresh perspective to the issues, and increases the credibility of, and receptivity to, responses. To these ends, we recommend that police departments form a task force to address racially biased policing and the perceptions thereof.

A task force should be considered advisory to the agency executive and comprise 15 to 25 people representing both the department and the community. In selecting community members, emphasis should be given to those most concerned with police racial bias. The task force should include representatives from the jurisdiction's various minority groups, as well as representatives from civil rights groups. Police personnel selected for the task force should represent the chief and all other departmental levels, particularly patrol. If applicable, a representative from the police union should also participate.

In designating the makeup of the task force, the agency executive should keep in mind that he or she will hear from critics within and outside the agency regarding the problem and potential remedies. The choice is either to have them participate in developing constructive solutions, or to wait and hear their critiques after the work is done. We recommend the former.

The task force could approach their work using a collaborative problem-solving model. They should start by defining and analyzing the issues in the jurisdiction. They can discuss perceived issues among themselves, as well as collect information through community focus group discussions, surveys, department data, and other means. Discussions and surveys, in particular, not only define the issues, but also allow citizens to vent their frustrations and be heard. Once the issues have been defined, the stage has been set for the critically important process of developing responses. Again, this should be a collaborative process, with both citizens and police personnel deciding what areas require action, and what those actions will be.

Lowell, Mass., provides an example of a promising police-community initiative. There, one of the focus groups for the PERF project has been transformed into a police-citizen task force. Citizens and police officers had initially met to discuss racially biased policing, particularly as it might occur during vehicle stops. After some finger-pointing, raised voices, citizen accusations, and defensiveness on both sides, the group started to develop ways to resolve the particular problems they had identified. On their own, without prompting from the facilitator, they agreed that they needed to meet regularly to continue the process of sharing, listening and resolving problems. The chief has continued the group as the "Race Relations Council." They have met several times and have come up with new ideas regarding police training and police-citizen communication. The mayor reports that this council is "the best thing that has happened in Lowell in a long time."

Chicago's work also reflects police-citizen collaboration to address police racial bias and the perceptions thereof. Chicago's police superintendent sponsored a series of forums for police and minority community residents. Community activists were recruited to join the police department in looking for solutions to racial tensions and addressing concerns about police racial bias. Department staff of all ranks were also invited to participate. Before the first forum convened, participants were surveyed for their opinions about racially biased policing and the department's strengths and weaknesses regarding minority outreach, and for their ideas about how to improve police-minority relations and resolve issues.

An independent facilitator (PERF Executive Director Chuck Wexler) moderated the initial sessions. During this first forum, community members shared their thoughts, experiences and concerns in the morning, and police staff were asked to listen and hold their responses until later in the day. Lunch was structured as a mixer, with informal discussions. In the afternoon, police staff shared their thoughts and reactions to the morning session, and the citizens were instructed to listen and not respond. During the final session of the day, all participants joined in a discussion of the issues and ideas raised earlier. Subsequent, ongoing discussions have identified specific actions to be taken by both the police and community members to address the issues raised.[1]

*Recommendation: Police departments should organize police-citizen task forces to identify how the jurisdiction can effectively respond to racially biased policing and the perceptions thereof.*

Effective outreach involves more than police-citizen engagement on the topic of race. Police departments should have long-term, sustained programs for reaching out to minority communities.

---

[1] Without accountability and short-term wins, this process runs the risk of being reduced to empty promises, making participants feel it is just a half-hearted attempt to appease the community.

## CONTEMPORARY AND PROGRESSIVE APPROACHES TO DEVELOPING STRONG RELATIONSHIPS WITH MINORITY COMMUNITIES

PERF used the survey and follow-up interviews with police departments across the country to identify innovative approaches for engaging minority communities. These approaches can be grouped into the following five categories:

- dialogue,
- feedback,
- services and visibility,
- immigrant outreach, and
- minority group participation.

Below we describe both contemporary and progressive approaches that fall within those categories. Contemporary approaches are conventional—known to and used by many police commanders. They are very viable methods for building strong police-community relations. Progressive approaches aren't as well known, but also hold great promise for enhancing police-community relations.

### Dialogue

Increased dialogue between minority groups and police personnel can build trust and respect, and identify areas where action is needed. Dialogue, however, is limited in that it does not necessarily lead to action. While it is necessary for outreach, it is not sufficient alone.

*Contemporary* dialogue might occur in

- sessions of police chief advisory boards (either one board with members from several minority communities, or several boards, one for each community);
- chaplain or faith programs involving minority clergy;
- radio and TV shows with call-ins; and
- forums or meetings.

*Progressive* dialogue might occur in

- beat meetings that are integral to joint community-police problem-solving;
- facilitated discussions (with a neutral, third-party moderator), which increase police and resident accountability for following up on agreed-upon actions; and
- study circles, which are structured to include three steps: organization of the community, identification of areas of mutual police-citizen concern and agreement, and action taken by both the police and minority groups.

## Feedback Solicitation

Soliciting feedback from minority citizens provides opportunities for traditionally underrepresented voices to be heard, sending the message that the police value minorities' input.

*Contemporary* feedback solicitation might include

- an open-door policy on the part of the police chief, to allow minority groups to discuss their concerns; and
- police minority-liaison positions with access to command staff (such access ensures that community feedback reaches those who can make changes in department operations).

*Progressive* feedback solicitation might include

- focused sampling of minority citizens in satisfaction surveys; and
- provision of complaint forms or placement of report-takers in nonpolice settings in predominantly minority communities.

## Services and Visibility

Police officers participate in a wide variety of community activities unrelated to traditional law enforcement to make police accessible and approachable and create opportunities for positive interactions between officers and community residents. Many of these are focused on minority communities.

*Contemporary* services and visibility might include

- attending community festivals;
- providing crime prevention assistance, such as engraving valuables, educating citizens about personal safety, facilitating block and neighborhood meetings, and supplying information about local crime patterns;
- sponsoring police athletic leagues;
- participating in mentoring programs; and
- engaging in joint police-community activities, such as cleanup efforts.

*Progressive* services and visibility might include

- opening youth centers;
- developing prostitution-prevention programs;
- creating community gardens; and
- providing tutoring.

While progressive, these services and visibility initiatives are not necessarily identified or developed in partnership with residents.

### Immigrant Outreach

While the national discussion on "racial profiling" has largely focused on black and Hispanic citizens, other minority groups are also at risk of racially biased policing or the perceptions thereof. In particular, many American cities are experiencing growth in new immigrant communities, communities with unique issues regarding how to relate to the police. Immigrant outreach efforts create means for communication between police and new immigrants.

*Contemporary* immigrant outreach efforts might include

- hiring bilingual officers and/or providing language training for officers working in immigrant communities; and

- staffing police minority-liaison positions with officers of the same ethnic background as the residents
  they serve.

*Progressive* immigrant outreach efforts might include
- inviting immigrant community representatives to
  educate the police about the community's customs,
  cultures, language, and public safety issues; and
- educating immigrant community residents about
  American police practices, local policies and how
  to access police services (for example, some police
  departments are sending officers to places where
  new immigrants congregate, such as driver's education classes, English-as-a-Second-Language classes
  and citizenship classes, to provide information).

## Minority Group Participation
Minority group participation ranges from limited, sometimes
passive, involvement in department-sponsored events to active involvement in advising the department about police operations. This latter type of participation results in shared
responsibility for public safety.

*Contemporary* minority group participation might include

- presenting information during police academy and
  in-service training;
- getting involved in chaplain programs;
- going on police ride-alongs; and
- joining citizens' police academies.

Progressive approaches create opportunities for minorities
to influence police operations, help develop policies affecting
police operations and/or oversee how policies are implemented
(as with citizen complaint review boards).

*Progressive* minority group participation might include
joining

- use-of-force and complaint review boards;
- hiring and promotion boards;

- curriculum review boards;
- policy review and policy development teams; and
- police-citizen task forces to address racially biased policing and the perceptions thereof.

*Recommendation: Police departments should use a combination of contemporary and progressive approaches to provide multiple opportunities for minority group interactions with the police.*

Below are examples of progressive approaches that police departments responding to the PERF survey have taken to develop stronger relationships with minority communities. They are intended to provide inspiration, and can be tailored to a jurisdiction's individual needs.

## Dialogue
*Study Circles Promote Goal-Oriented Discussions About Police-Community Relations*
Supported by the Study Circles Resource Center, the Buffalo (N.Y.) Police Department is engaging a diverse group of community members to form study circles, which are small, facilitated group sessions that use a structured dialogue process to address issues of police-community relations. The purpose of the dialogues is to identify areas for improvement about which citizens and police both agree, and about which they are in agreement regarding needed responses. (The study circle process is designed to capitalize on areas of existing agreement, not to achieve consensus where none currently exists.) Study circles serve to break down barriers between participants, enhancing relationships so that productive exchanges will continue after the formal process ends.

## Feedback Solicitation
*Task Force Seeks and Acts on Community Input*
After hearing that minorities were dissatisfied with the handling of misconduct complaints, the Kalamazoo (Mich.) Department of Public Safety set up a task force composed of residents from all identified minority communities. Based on task force recommendations regarding necessary and desired features of

a new complaint system, the department developed a new system and established a citizen review board.

*Community Police Council Brings Citizen Concerns to Police Attention*
The mayor of Albany, N.Y., formed a Community Police Council for citizens to share information with the police. The council includes minority and white residents representing neighborhood associations and business improvement districts. Council members identify community concerns about quality-of-life issues and police conduct.

## Services and Visibility
*Police Department Provides Services to Recent Immigrants*
The St. Paul (Minn.) Police Department is working to empower recent immigrant families—Russian, Vietnamese, Laotian, Cambodian, Hmong, and Ethiopian—living in public housing. Services include counseling, victim assistance, tutoring, advocacy and referral, gang prevention training, crisis intervention, translation, and after-school programs. A dedicated staff of one sergeant, seven officers, three community liaison representatives/interpreters, and six summer youth workers are engaged full time in serving these immigrant communities.

*Problem-Solving Results in Services for Youth*
In Adams County, Colo., community policing has been instrumental in enhancing the relationship between the police and numerous minority communities. Through interactions with citizens, officers determined that the lack of after-school activities for Hmong youth was leading to community disorder. The police department established and runs a youth center. The center has promoted improved relationships between the police and minority communities, and even rival gang members are forming positive relationships with each other as a result of their involvement with the center.

*Problem-Solving Leads to Services for Migrant Workers*
The Washington State Patrol engages in collaborative problem-solving with community members to address issues troopers

have identified in areas throughout the state. For example, troopers in eastern Washington farming communities identified various traffic safety problems relating to Spanish-speaking migrant workers. As a result, Spanish-speaking troopers have been instructing workers to wear seat belts and providing information on how to obtain driver's licenses. In addition, the troopers have talked with farmers about training migrant employees before allowing them to transport equipment and produce in trucks.

## Immigrant Outreach
*Joint Effort Breaks Down Barriers Between Police and New Immigrants*
An El Cajon, Calif., police captain observed that the Kurdish immigrant community was growing, and that the immigrants were in increasing contact with local police. The captain reached out to Kurdish religious and cultural leaders from the Coptic Christian and Shiite and Sunni Moslem communities. The police and Kurdish community leaders invited school district leaders to join them in a series of meetings in which participants could jointly identify issues and barriers, and develop programs to address them. The police, school district leaders and Kurdish community representatives are continuing to talk, breaking down barriers to communication and enabling more effective policing in the community.

*Citizen Council and Police Provide Support to Immigrants*
The Central Weed and Seed Citizen Advisory Council (CAC) in Seattle's East Precinct has identified East African immigrants as a growing population there. The East African community is facing numerous cultural and social challenges. CAC is trying to bridge gaps and open discussions about safety, social, school, and family assimilation issues. A Seattle police officer has been assigned as the community's liaison officer, and he will work with residents to address such community issues as follows:

- the difficulties in locating translators;
- the need for crime prevention and gang awareness training for parents;

- the need to translate city documents (e.g., crime prevention, school and community police academy materials);
- the lack of understanding of the city's process for accessing assistance/resources; and
- the religious barriers to immigrants' working with police (e.g., women at home alone can't let male officers into the residence).

## Minority Group Participation
*Community Oversight Creates Trust and Openness*
The Phoenix Police Department includes residents on use-of-force review boards and on hiring and promotion boards. In addition, a use-of-force forum has allowed community members to learn about officers' decision-making processes during critical incidents. The department has sought community input in developing cultural awareness training for officers, and has instructed community members about the police culture. Phoenix's police chief visits with minorities in their homes to listen to their concerns, and has advisory boards representing African-Americans, gays and lesbians, senior citizens, Native Americans, Hispanics, and Asians.

*Police-Community Meetings Lead to Action*
In Denver, representatives from locally based advocacy groups (e.g., the NAACP and the American Civil Liberties Union) and neighborhood organizations have joined with the police department to hold a series of community meetings on racial profiling. Community members and line officers have collaborated to develop policies and procedures related to racial profiling, a protocol for data collection, police training in cultural diversity, police retraining in Fourth Amendment concepts and mandates, and training for citizens regarding police contacts.

*Facilitated Meetings Engage Diverse Groups in Policy Changes*
In Spokane, Wash., an ongoing series of facilitated meetings involves a wide range of community stakeholders, including concerned citizens, police personnel, the NAACP, the U.S.

Attorney's Office, defense attorneys, the local Commission on African-American Affairs, the Native Americans Project, the Asian Community Coalition, the American Civil Liberties Union, the Police Officer's Guild, the Department of Justice Community Relations Division, the city council, and the FBI. The meetings focus on three main issues: educating the public about police procedures, collecting data on the race of individuals stopped, and improving community access to the civilian complaint system. As of this writing, the group is in the brainstorming phase; they expect policy changes to result from the process.

## CONCLUSION

Police departments should include minority community outreach in their efforts to address racially biased policing and the perceptions thereof. Improved relations between the police and minorities will increase officers' ability to provide high-quality policing services to all the residents in their jurisdiction. The ultimate results will be mutual trust and respect, and shared responsibility for public safety.

# Data Collection on Citizens' Race/Ethnicity To Address Racially Biased Policing and the Perceptions Thereof

## INTRODUCTION

Since "racial profiling" has become a national issue, many jurisdictions have started collecting data on the race/ethnicity of citizens stopped and/or searched by police. This practice reflects accountability, openness and sound management. It is interesting, however, that data collection became known early on as *the way* for police agencies to respond, with very little attention given to other ways agencies might address both racially biased policing and the perceptions thereof.

There are pros *and* cons to data collection; thus PERF neither recommends nor opposes such efforts. Instead, we believe that each agency should decide whether or not to collect data based on those pros and cons, as well as on political, community, organizational, and financial factors.

In this chapter, we discuss the advantages of data collection for information development and management, accountability and trust-building. However, we also note the limitations of data collection, and attempt to reduce to a realistic level the very high nationwide expectations regarding what data can tell us. For those agencies that are required or choose to collect data, we provide recommendations regarding what activities to target for data collection, and what data elements to include.

Further, we outline the constraints associated with data analysis and interpretation, to promote responsible use of results. Our purpose is to ensure that agencies that collect data do so in a way that increases the positive potential and minimizes the negative. Particularly important is that data collection be associated with sound analysis and interpretation; without strong processes in place for analysis and interpretation, data collection can be more harmful than beneficial.[1]

## WHETHER OR NOT TO COLLECT DATA

Again, there are pros *and* cons to collecting data as a response to racially biased policing and the perceptions thereof. Whether the positives outweigh the negatives, or vice versa, depends on the myriad factors within each individual jurisdiction.

### Arguments in Favor of Data Collection

*Data Collection Helps Agencies To Determine Whether*
*Racially Biased Policing Is a Problem in the Jurisdiction*
Eighteen percent of the respondents to the PERF survey reported that their agencies had "initiated the collection of new data or the analysis of existing data for the purpose of assessing the race/ethnicity of citizens encountered, stopped and/or arrested," and many more agencies appear to be contemplating this option. A common motivation is the desire to determine the nature and extent of racially biased policing. By collecting data, agencies can advance the debate from stories and anecdotes to empirical evidence, and implement targeted responses based on the results. Departments can identify agency policies or practices that lead to racially biased policing, and use the data to stimulate further inquiry into whether an officer's behavior is biased. Departments can also evaluate their progress in reducing racially biased policing over time. Collecting information on police racial bias reflects solid management practices, serving as a department-level assessment of a critical national problem.

---

[1] This is reflected in the International Association of Chiefs of Police (2001) statement on "Traffic Stops and Data Collection": "[T]he IACP will only support data collection legislation that ensures that an impartial and scientifically sound methodology will be used for evaluating collected data."

*Data Collection Helps Agencies To Convey a Commitment to Unbiased Policing*
Data collection conveys important messages to both the community and agency personnel: that biased policing will not be tolerated, and that officers are accountable to the citizens they serve. The initiation of data collection lets citizens know that the police chief is committed to addressing community concerns. It also may deter unnecessary and/or illegal stops of citizens on the part of line personnel.

*Data Collection Helps Agencies To "Get Ahead of the Curve"*
Some chiefs who responded to our survey or spoke with staff initiated data collection within their departments in anticipation of mandates (e.g., state legislation) that they do so. These chiefs wanted to develop protocols that might become the models for their mandates, rather than have protocols imposed on them by authorities who might not have a full understanding of the issues and of agency procedures and information systems.

*Data Collection Helps Agencies To Effectively Allocate and Manage Department Resources*
The information gathered during data collection can be beneficial beyond the examination of racially biased policing. By learning about the quality and quantity of the stops made by personnel, an agency can better manage and allocate department resources.

### Arguments Against Data Collection[2]
*Data Collection Does Not Yield Valid Information Regarding the Nature and Extent of Racially Biased Policing*
Social science is not capable of providing valid answers to every question posed. Indeed, there are many chiefs who sincerely would like to gauge whether or not their departments engage in racially

---

[2] A number of the survey respondents reported they had chosen not to collect data or analyze existing data because racially biased policing was not a problem in their jurisdiction. While this may be true for some jurisdictions, an agency should not assume that it is without problems just because, for instance, it has few ethnic/racial minorities and/or has few citizen complaints

biased policing, but are concerned about whether cost-effective social science methods can produce the information they seek. Specifically, while agencies can have *reasonable* confidence in the data they collect from their officers regarding whom they stop, there are legitimate questions as to whether there are, at present, cost-effective methods for interpreting these data to reach valid, meaningful conclusions. As discussed more fully below, the challenge is to develop "benchmarks" or other standards by which to determine whether racially biased policing is indicated by, for instance, the fact that 25 percent of an agency's traffic stops are of Hispanics. In effect, the process of analysis and interpretation is one of trying to understand the full context of a stop (e.g., drivers' demographic makeup, enforcement activity including the assignment of field officers), and of identifying what factors within that context affect the police decision to, for instance, stop and search the citizen. This is a very challenging endeavor.

*Data Will Be Used To Harm the Agency or Its Personnel*
A related concern is that the data collected—despite the ambiguity surrounding their meaning—will be used to disparage or otherwise harm the agency or its personnel. Police executives have concerns that questionable data interpretations will be used irresponsibly by agency critics, including the media, and/

---

of biased policing. Regarding the nature of a jurisdiction's population, some emerging empirical evidence indicates that racially biased policing may be most prevalent in areas where racial/ethnic minorities are few (see, for example, Meehan and Ponder 2000). Regarding citizen complaints, most studying or working in the law enforcement field are aware that the frequency of citizen complaints may reflect the accessibility of, and citizen faith in, the complaint system as much as the behavior of officers on the streets. In other words, few or no complaints of racially biased policing may reflect either the lack of the practice or citizen reluctance to report it.

We believe police executives should be cautious in assuming they have no problems with racially biased policing and, instead, we set forth below more viable reasons that might prompt a jurisdiction to invest in alternative responses to data collection.

Also, the argument that data collection will have a negative effect because asking citizens what their race is will add tension to encounters is easily and appropriately handled by using an alternative method for identifying a person's race (e.g., officer's perception, driver's license information).

or used in lawsuits against the agency.[3] Some of the survey respondents reported they were not collecting data under the advice of agency counsel concerned that the data could be misinterpreted in legal actions, at great costs to the agency. Similar concerns pertain to agency personnel. Line officers have expressed great concern that data will be used against them in legal or disciplinary actions, despite legitimate questions as to the data's validity. When information linking disparate impact to a specific officer without explanation or interpretation is made public there can be significant harm to the officer.

### Data Collection May Impact Police Productivity, Morale and Workload

Another concern is that officers resentful of the implications of data collection, and concerned about the "results" of their own data, will suffer from lowered morale and decrease the enforcement activities associated with the data collection. For instance, officers may stop fewer traffic violators, resulting in decreased safety for drivers. Furthermore, data collection will require additional staff time for data processing and analysis.

### Police Resources Might Be More Effectively Used To Combat Racially Biased Policing and the Perceptions Thereof

Data collection may require not only additional staff time, but also other resources. For instance, survey respondents, when asked what resources they would need for data collection and analysis, indicated they might need new forms, computer hardware and software, additional personnel, and/or training and technical assistance. The agency executive, in discussions with citizen leaders, might, in fact, determine that data collection is an appropriate response, or may choose to target financial and staff resources to engage in minority community outreach, enhance supervision capabilities, improve citizen complaint processes, upgrade academy or in-service training, acquire in-car videos, and so forth.

---

[3] There are an increasing number of reports of defense attorneys' using such data in court cases.

## Summary

Police agencies can use data collection on the race/ethnicity of citizens with whom police engage to explore the prevalence and nature of racially biased policing, to show accountability to the citizens they serve, and to convey concern about this important national issue. If an agency undertakes data collection, it should inform citizens and the media about what the data can and cannot show.

The critical issue of racially biased policing and the perceptions thereof merits some agency resources. Because it is a critical human rights issue, agencies should expect to invest in effective prevention or remedial measures—ideally, with the financial support of local, state and/or federal government. Agency executives may responsibly choose to invest resources in responses other than data collection. (However, while rejecting a full-fledged data collection system, they might consider a small-scale and/or periodic data collection effort as one aspect of an overall assessment and response effort.)

*Recommendation: Police executives, in collaboration with citizen leaders should review the pros and cons of data collection and decide—in light of the agency's political, social, organizational, and financial situation—either to initiate data collection or to allocate available resources to other responses to racially biased policing and the perceptions thereof.*

## DATA COLLECTION PROTOCOL

In the previous section, we outlined the pros and cons of collecting data in response to concerns about police racial bias. For those agencies that decide or are required to collect data, we provide in this section recommendations for doing so. We base our recommendations on a review of existing reports—most notably, the recently released Justice Department publication, *A Resource Guide on Racial Profiling Data Collection Systems* (Ramirez, McDevitt and Farrell 2000)—the examination of nearly 150 data collection protocols from police agencies responding to our survey; and discussions of data collection with social scientists, executives, command staff, supervisors, and line officers in focus groups and other PERF forums for debate. Below we provide guidance regarding the following questions:

- On what law enforcement activities should agencies collect data?
- What information should agencies collect regarding those activities?
- How should agencies analyze and interpret the data?

We also discuss how and why a department should use a police-citizen task force to design the data collection protocol, and provide a list of the initial steps for setting up a system.

### Activities To Target for Data Collection

Figure 1 shows a series of concentric circles that represent the types of activities police departments might target for data col-

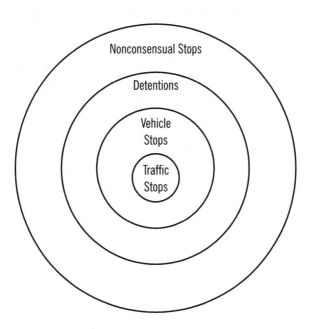

**Fig. 1. Activities that could be targeted for data collection**

lection. The smallest unit (and innermost circle) is *traffic stops*—that is, vehicle stops based only on traffic violations. The next circle denotes *all vehicle stops*—traffic stops and other investigative stops (including those for suspicious activity). The third circle represents vehicle stops as well as pedestrian stops that meet the legal definition of *detention*.[4] The outermost circle—*nonconsensual encounters*—includes all detentions, plus all police-initiated encounters (with either motorists or pedestrians) that do not amount to detentions. In other words, the outer circle includes cases in which an officer approaches and questions someone outside of the realm of a consensual encounter, but does not legally detain the person.

Below we discuss each of these target groups of activities.

*Traffic Stops*

Many agencies that are collecting data are focusing on traffic stops only. This might be considered sufficient because much of the discussion about "racial profiling" has focused on traffic stops, and, by virtue of their frequency, traffic stops hold the greatest potential for police racial bias, or perceptions of it, to occur. Traffic stops also likely represent the greatest number of pretext stops. Although focusing only on traffic stops means data are not collected for other, less visible, high-officer-discretion encounters, some social scientists argue that traffic stops can be used as a "sample" of activity for diagnosing whether an agency has a problem. Another advantage to collecting only traffic stop data pertains to the challenges associated with data analysis and interpretation. As discussed below, identifying "benchmarks" (that is, developing hypothetical comparison groups for purposes of analysis) for traffic stops is somewhat easier than for other categories of activities (though still a great challenge).

---

[4] Detentions require reasonable suspicion, and they occur when a reasonable person believes he or she is not free to go.

*Vehicle Stops*

Collecting data only for traffic stops excludes obtaining information about general investigative stops of motorists.[5] Since a major purpose for collecting data is to try to assess whether officers misuse their discretion when they target certain people for interventions, police agencies should seek to collect data on high-officer-discretion/low-visibility activities in which racial bias is most likely to occur—as with vehicle stops. The disadvantages of extending data collection beyond traffic stops to all vehicle stops are the additional logistics, staff time and costs associated with doing so. In addition, extending data collection to all vehicle stops increases the challenges associated with identifying appropriate comparison populations for purposes of analysis.[6]

*Detentions*

Collecting data on all detentions—including traffic, vehicle and pedestrian stops—increases the advantages and disadvantages discussed above. By adding pedestrian stops, an agency is including activities that also have great potential for police racial bias, or the perceptions of it. For some agencies, pedestrian stops are barely visible—generally beyond supervisors' observation, and resulting in no paperwork unless a stop produces evidence. If racially biased policing is occurring, these stops provide the opportunity to misuse discretion, at times resulting in grave civil rights abuses of citizens on the street. Another advantage of including pedestrian stops is that officers who do not con-

---

[5] Again, we are using the term *traffic stops* to denote stops made for violations of motor vehicle laws. *Vehicle stops* include traffic stops, but also include other types of motorist stops—most notably, investigative stops (e.g., when a driver matches a suspect description).

[6] As discussed more fully below, a major factor in interpreting these data is trying to determine whom the police would stop in an unbiased world. This is challenging enough when one considers only traffic stops. It involves determining who is at risk for a traffic stop based on driving behavior, enforcement activity and so forth. By adding investigative stops, we have to additionally estimate who is at risk for being pulled over for, for instance, matching a suspect description.

duct vehicle stops will also be held accountable. Again, though, this additional data collection adds logistical issues, time and costs, and yet another challenge to "benchmarking."[7]

### Nonconsensual Encounters

By *nonconsensual encounters,* we refer to instances in which an officer engages a citizen in a manner not invited by the citizen, but that does not amount to a legal detention (i.e., a reasonable person would believe that he or she was free to go). Again, the advantages and disadvantages discussed above are multiplied. Collecting data on these encounters brings police activities with great potential for racial bias, or perceptions of it, under review. However, adding this information again increases the problems associated with logistics, the challenges in defining the target activities (i.e., which encounters are nonconsensual), and benchmarking.

### Summary

Determining which data to collect involves balancing the need for information on high-discretion/low-visibility stops against considerations of time, officer safety, convenience, community priorities and resources. *In considering this balance, we recommend that if agencies collect data, they collect data on all vehicle stops.* This includes all detentions and arrests of motorists, including stops for traffic violations, criminal violations and suspicious persons/activities. It does not include pedestrian stops or nonconsensual encounters that do not amount to detentions. We believe that, overall, by collecting data on vehicle stops, departments may achieve the appropriate balance between producing information and expending resources. However, since the factors related to this balance will vary across agencies, we believe an agency collecting data may responsibly choose to target only traffic stops or, possibly, *initiate* its system by focusing only on traffic stops, and then, over time, include vehicle stops. A department

---

[7] In terms of benchmarking, the added challenge is that the relevant ideal "comparison group" for purposes of analysis and interpretation comprises those people at risk of being stopped in a vehicle or on foot in an unbiased world. We discuss the issue of benchmarking more fully below.

certainly can consider data collection on pedestrian stops, as well (that is, expand to detention data), depending on the particular issues raised in its jurisdiction.

*Recommendation: If agencies are mandated or choose to collect data, they should consider targeting all vehicle stops.*

For those activities targeted for data collection (e.g., vehicle stops), the agency should gather information on *all incidents*, regardless of disposition. This point is best conveyed through an example: Some agencies have decided to collect data on only those traffic stops that result in citations. This decision may be based on the desire to simplify data collection (i.e., rely on existing forms, such as citations), or the departments might argue that traffic stops resulting in official sanctions are of more concern than those that lead to *no disposition*. In fact, agencies should pay due attention to stops that *do not* result in official sanctions because, while the group of *no disposition* stops may include a number of fortunate drivers who could have been issued tickets but were not, the group could just as well include a number of drivers for which there were no legally justifiable reasons for the stops.[8]

As a final point, departments should review the existing data relevant to their many and varied activities (beyond those discussed here)—data that might provide a more comprehensive picture of how their services and law enforcement activities disparately impact different racial or ethnic communities. In other words, even if a department collects data on all vehicle stops, it is important to keep in mind that vehicle stops represent just one aspect of their work in the community. Existing relevant information departments might review—if available by citizens' race/ethnicity—could include data on victims served, complaints filed, citizens present at police-community meetings, youth involvement in police-sponsored activities, and residential search warrants executed. Such information could provide a broader sense of how the agency engages its diverse communities.

---

[8] One department protocol we reviewed requires that all *no disposition* stops pass through an extra level of review.

## Data Elements To Include

Just as agencies need to balance the need for information against limits on resources in determining which activities to collect data on, the same considerations apply to selecting which data elements to include. On the one hand, an agency might develop a system that has so few incident data elements that it is essentially worthless for assessing racially biased policing. On the other hand, an agency might develop a system that is so cumbersome that even the best officers think twice about engaging in the targeted activities.

*Recommendation: Agencies that choose or are mandated to collect data should include the data elements and response options listed below.*

### Table 1. Proposed Data Elements and Coding

1) Time/Date
2) Location: Beat, division, block, intersection, etc.
3) Age: <18, 18–29; 30–39; 40–49; 50+
4) Gender: Male/Female
5) Race:
>   White
>   Black/African American
>   Asian/Pacific Islander
>   Native American/Eskimo/Aleut
>   Middle Eastern/East Indian
6) Hispanic/Latino: Yes/No
7) Does citizen live in metropolitan area defined by U.S. Census? Yes/No
8) Reason for Stop
>   Reactive Stop (e.g., call for service, special detail such as roadblock) vs. Self-Initiated Stop (e.g., proactive vehicle or pedestrian stop)
>   Vehicle Code Violation:
>>      Red Light/Stop Sign
>>      Speed [_____ mph over limit]
>>      Lane violation
>>      Commercial vehicle
>>      Following too closely
>>      Failure to signal
>>      Other moving violation
>>      Hazardous equipment
>>      Seat belt
>>      Other nonmoving violation

Penal Code Violation:
    Nuisance (related to quality of life)
    Vice
    Property crime
    Violent crime
    Violation of local ordinance
    BOLO/Person wanted
    Suspicious circumstances

9) Disposition:
    Arrest
    Ticket/Citation
    Verbal warning
    Written warning
    No action

10) Length of Stop: 0–15 min.; 16–30 min.; 31–60 min.; 61+

11) Were citizen's characteristics observable before stop? Yes/No

12) Comment Section: [allows for explanations for variables, if needed]

13) Employee ID: [Or at least beat, division, and/or unit]

SEARCH VARIABLES

14) Was a search conducted? Yes/No

15) What was searched?
    If just collecting on vehicle stops:
        Vehicle
        Personal effects
        Driver
        Passenger(s)
    If collecting on both vehicle/pedestrian:
        Person: pedestrian, driver, passenger
        Vehicle
        Building/Residence
        Property/Personal effects

16) Authority to Search?
    Consent
    Reasonable suspicion—weapon
    Incident to arrest
    Probable cause
    Inventory
    Plain view
    Other

17) Search Results: Positive/Negative

18) What was recovered?
    Currency
    Weapon (or "gun" and "other weapon")
    Stolen property
    Illegal drugs/Drug paraphernalia
    Other
19) Optional: Additional details

Again, we base our recommendations on a review of reports on the topic, an examination of data collection protocol, and discussions with experts.[9]

The rationale for the inclusion of each element follows and, where appropriate, the justification for the items or responses we recommend within elements (e.g., age and race categories). The key to selecting data elements is to measure not only *whom* police are engaging, but also the circumstances and context of the stop. In effect, we are trying to collect "circumstantial" data to tell us the real reasons citizens are being stopped—which should reflect the motivations of the officers and/or the impact of agency policies and practices. The contextual data officers collect about stops, along with the "benchmarking" information as described below, will help determine whether and to what extent race/ethnicity is a motivating factor.

**Reasons To Include Specific Data Elements**
The data elements of *time, date* and *location* allow for assessments of racially biased policing by time and geography. Driving behavior can be expected to vary greatly across these variables. For instance, drivers—even drivers with varying types of behaviors—can be expected in specific areas on specific days (e.g., college students driving to the football stadium on weekends, factory workers traveling to and from work mornings and evenings).

---

[9] Agencies that cannot accommodate a system that includes all the variables we propose might exclude the search variables, but should maintain the initial element: *Was a search conducted?*

Police should collect data on perceived *age* and *gender* of those stopped because these characteristics correlate with allegations of greater police abuse of power (e.g., *young* black *males* are presumed to be frequent targets of "racial profiling") and with driving behavior.

We suggest separate items for *race* and *Hispanic/Latino* so that a jurisdiction can retain the option of comparing their stop data with census data that also separate these variables. The particular "codes" (e.g., *white, black/African-American*) are consistent with the census, except for the addition of *Middle Eastern/East Indian*. While agencies can customize these codes to their jurisdiction's population, we advise them to retain the ability to recombine categories during analysis to match census categories. In the course of customization, departments should avoid producing too many different response categories, as such coding can be more unwieldy than useful.

Vigorous debates among PERF project staff on the issue of how to measure race made it clear that this task raises not just social science questions, but political/moral ones as well. Most of the protocols we reviewed suggested that race/ethnicity be gauged by the officer's perceptions, reflecting a strictly social science perspective.[10] This method of measurement reflects the research question posed by these data collection systems. While there are a number of reasons to adopt a data collection system (see the pros set forth at the beginning of the chapter), the major social science reason is to determine whether officers are using race/ethnicity inappropriately in deciding with whom to engage. To the extent that officers make stopping decisions based on race, they do so based on their *perceptions* of race, not on the basis of driver's license information that they have not yet seen. That these perceptions of race are likely erroneous in some unknown number of incidents does not negate the fact that the perceptions are the valid measure of race in light of the research question. For example, an officer who thought the person he stopped was white may have in fact stopped a citizen

---

[10] Asking people to self-report their race/ethnicity may be offensive and/or otherwise create or escalate tension in an encounter.

whose driver's license indicates he is Hispanic. In terms of try-ing to gauge whether or not the officer is biased, his or her perception is key. (Of course, who is stopped is only one vari-able to consider in this assessment of whether racially biased policing occurs.)

While some staff, for the above-stated reasons, advocated that race be measured through officers' perceptions, others advo-cated that officers glean the information from driver's licenses. As its base, this latter stance reflects two key political/moral arguments: that officers should not be put in the position of making this sensitive distinction, and that other government entities should share responsibility and accountability. Regard-ing the latter, in the realm of shared responsibility, it would require that states that have removed race/ethnicity informa-tion from driver's licenses and other state identification cards again reexamine this decision to facilitate and support officers' data collection. The argument becomes even more compelling in states that require data collection on the part of agencies.[11] This viewpoint is supported by an IACP resolution that "urges states to incorporate race and ethnicity as a data element and print it on the driver's licenses to facilitate the capture and ac-curate recording of this information."[12]

We recommend including data on *where the citizen lives* (e.g., within or outside of city limits) to facilitate analysis. For agencies that use census data for interpreting department data, including residence will allow them to develop a subsample of incidents involving only residents for the purpose of benchmarking those data against residential census data. In other words, with this information, an agency could compare the demographics of city residents stopped (i.e., exclude non-residents stopped) against the census data demographics for

---

[11] If information on race/ethnicity were available on driver's licenses, then agency executives would at least have the option of choosing between the various methods of measuring race/ethnicity.

[12] IACP resolution, "Incorporation of Racial Background as a Data Element on Drivers' Licenses," adopted at the 106th Annual Conference, Charlotte, N.C., Nov. 3, 1999.

all city residents. The wording of this item on a department's form (e.g., "Does citizen live in the city? In the county?") should reflect the jurisdiction's relevant *metropolitan area* (e.g., city, county) as defined by the census. To obtain this information, the officer could use the citizen's driver's license or inquire.

Critically important in data collection is information regarding the *reason for a stop*. Ramirez, McDevitt and Farrell (2000) refer to this as "one of the most important pieces of information that will be collected" and stress the importance of developing a single or several variables to measure *discretion* (p. 48). The greatest potential for racially biased policing—at least in terms of *whom* police engage (as opposed to *how they interact* with the person during engagement)—occurs in high-discretion stops. For instance, officers have and exercise great discretion in deciding whether to pull someone over for failing to signal. In contrast, officers have less discretion in responding to someone who runs a red light at a major intersection. Thus, a finding that a particular officer gives 80 percent of his or her "failing to signal" citations to blacks can be viewed differently than a finding that an officer gives 80 percent of his or her red-light citations to blacks. The latter is less likely to indicate possible biased policing than the former, which should prompt additional review of the citations' circumstances/context (e.g., the racial composition of the area being policed).

The variable *reactive/self-initiated* is an important measure of discretion. A *reactive* stop is one precipitated by a call for police service or other external demand (e.g., supervisor direction, direct citizen contact). Supervisor direction could include an officer's placement on a special detail (e.g., hot-spot enforcement, drunken-driving roadblock, special gun initiative). A stop an officer conducts solely on his or her own initiative (e.g., a traffic stop while on patrol) would be coded *self-initiated*. With this variable analyses can differentiate between the incidents in which the officers select whom they will engage and those in which they engage in response to calls for service or assignment. The former is more relevant to an assessment of racially biased policing.

The *reason for the stop* allows an officer to indicate whether the stop is for a *vehicle code, penal code* or *local ordinance violation;* a *BOLO/person wanted;* or *suspicious circumstances.* The purpose of including subcategories within *vehicle code violations* and *penal code violations* is, again, to measure discretion. Thus, for instance, stops for *red-light violations* reflect less discretion than those for *lane-changing violations.* Similarly, detentions or arrests for nuisance crimes reflect far more discretion than those for violent crimes. Asking for *recorded speed above the posted limit* provides another measure of discretion, as officers have more discretion in stopping someone going just a few miles an hour over the speed limit, and less if someone is speeding quite dangerously.

The codes we propose for various *dispositions of stops* allow for an additional potential measure of equitable vs. disparate treatment. Beyond data collection on *whom* police stop, another important question is whether they treat those they stop differently based on their race/ethnicity. To begin to capture this information, we suggest *arrest, ticket/citation, verbal warning, written warning,* or *no action* (or *no disposition*) for the codes. *No action* would include releasing a person following a determination that he or she was not, in fact, the person being sought.[13] It is interesting to note that we identified several departments that changed their policies to discontinue verbal warnings in traffic stops. This was done to deter unnecessary stops (including, of course, those based on race) and to facilitate use of existing forms for data collection (i.e., there was an existing form for every other disposition—citation, arrest, written warning). For the same reasons, agencies should consider discontinuing verbal warnings—weighing the pros and cons of exercising this option.

*Length of stop* data also provide a potential measure of equitable vs. disparate treatment. With these data, an agency can explore whether the length of stops varies by race/ethnicity ("controlling" for relevant variables, such as the reason for the stop).

---

[13] Remember, *no action* should not necessarily be presumed to reflect benign law enforcement.

In our focus groups, many officers expressed great frustration at accusations of racial bias, and lamented that they were so accused even when it was clearly impossible for them to *discern driver characteristics before a stop.* Thus, we include a data element allowing officers to report this information, which has significant relevance to an assessment of whether or not stopping decisions are based on race/ethnicity.[14] Specifically, the officer would indicate whether or not the citizen's characteristics were observable before the stop.

A *comment section* would allow officers to note any other circumstances or contextual information that they thought relevant to their decision-making.

A controversial aspect of data collection concerns linking data to *individual officers.* In some jurisdictions, executives have implemented systems with the promise that only aggregate information would be analyzed, with no data linked to individual officers. This reflects officers' concerns that they will be disciplined or stigmatized based on data that may be invalid or misleading; they fear that individual-level data could become evidence in civil, criminal or disciplinary actions against them. Related to these concerns, some chiefs' decisions not to link the stop data to officer identifiers have reflected their desire to maintain the full trust of their personnel and thus increase the likelihood of obtaining their support for data collection.

On the other hand, many officers and command staff in our focus groups stated that "if, indeed, racial profiling occurs," it is not widespread, but rather committed by a small number of officers. Whether it is, in fact, "just a few" or, instead, a large number of officers, a data collection system that is implemented with the true intent of assessing and responding to racially biased policing should have the capacity to identify *potentially* problematic officers. The word *potentially* reflects an important point about how data should be used. These data cannot

---

[14] An oft-stated concern is that some officers will understate the frequency with which they can discern motorists' characteristics. Departments could attempt to identify those officers by comparing officers who have similar assignments (e.g., night shift, day shift) with regard to their results on this element.

prove *causation*—only *correlation*. It is critically important for command staff to understand that their data collection system cannot rule out all competing hypotheses that might explain why data for an officer indicate disproportionate stops (or searches or arrests) of racial/ethnic minorities. The data should be used only as *one indicator* of a potential problem, and prompt further exploration. That is, the data should be just one aspect of an "early warning system" for racially biased policing. Policies and statutes that link individual officer "results" directly to disciplinary measures are unfair and misguided.

*Recommendation: Police departments should consider the pros and cons of linking data to officer identity. If a department chooses not to collect data with links to individual officers, the data should be linked to units of the department—such as assignment or beat.*

Assessing racially biased vs. equitable policing requires looking not only at *whom* police engage, but also at *what happens* during the engagement. For instance, some studies on vehicle stops have identified even greater racial disparities with regard to who is searched than with who is stopped.[15] Because searches are high-discretion/low-visibility activities that have great potential for police abuse or perceptions of abuse, departments collecting data should include search data in their collection system. Ramirez, McDevitt and Farrell (2000:51) provide these arguments for including search data:

> Although it may seem easier to omit search information from the process, it serves two valuable functions. First, search information provides local jurisdictions with a sense of the quantity

---

[15] See, for example, Harris, D. (1999b), "The Stories, the Statistics and the Law: Why Driving While Black Matters," *Minnesota Law Review* 84(2):1–45; San Diego Police Department (2000), "Vehicle Stop Study, Mid-Year Report," Sept. 21; State of New Jersey (1999), "Interim Report of the State Police Review Team Regarding Allegations of Racial Profiling," April 20; and Bureau of Justice Statistics (2001), *Contacts Between Police and the Public: Findings From the 1999 National Survey*, Washington, D.C.: U.S. Department of Justice.

and quality of searches being conducted, the characteristics of those searches and their productivity. Productivity refers to the number of searches that result in arrests or seizures, the nature of those arrests and the quality of the seizures. Such information allows local jurisdictions to appropriately allocate resources to productive search techniques. Second, information about searches allows departments to assess whether certain groups are disproportionally targeted for searches.

The form should record *whether or not a search (including a frisk) was conducted*, and solicit additional information regarding searches. (Since searches are fairly rare, in most cases, this section will be blank.) Responses for *What was searched?* are *vehicle, personal effects, driver,* and/or *passenger(s)*. For those agencies that choose to collect data on both vehicle and pedestrian stops, we propose responses of *person* [specifying *pedestrian, driver* and/or *passenger(s)*], *vehicle, building/residence,* and/or *property/personal effects*.

An item on *authority to search* will not only provide important contextual information for analysis, but also will remind officers of the legal limits on their ability to search. The responses include *consent, reasonable suspicion—weapon, incident to arrest, probable cause, inventory,* and *plain view*. Collecting data on search outcome (as either *positive* or *negative*) and on what was recovered (i.e., *currency, weapon, stolen property, illegal drugs/drug paraphernalia, other*) allows for an agency assessment of search productivity. The results of these analyses may become the content for training.[16]

---

[16] For instance, empirical data have challenged many police officers' belief that searches of African-Americans are "positive" more often than searches of whites. See, for example, Harris, D. (1999b), "The Stories, the Statistics and the Law: Why Driving While Black Matters."

## DATA ANALYSIS AND INTERPRETATION

In discussing the pros and cons of data collection, we have conveyed many police executives' concern about a data collection system's ability to produce valid answers to even the most sincere questions about the nature and extent of racially biased policing. This reflects the concern about social science methods' ability to aid in assessing whether there is a causal main effect between citizen race/ethnicity and police behavior. To draw definitive conclusions regarding stop data that *indicate* disproportionate engagement of racial/ethnic minorities, we would need to be able to identify and disentangle the impact of race from legitimate factors that might reasonably explain individual and aggregated decisions to stop, search and otherwise engage people. This is not possible. As stated in a U.S. General Accounting Office report (2000), because of methodological challenges, "we cannot determine whether the rate at which African-Americans or other minorities are stopped is disproportionate to the rate at which they commit violations that put them at risk of being stopped" (p. 18).

In an attempt to rule out alternative factors, agencies strive to develop comparison groups against which to evaluate their vehicle stop data. Specifically, agencies try to develop comparison groups that reflect the demographic makeup of groups at risk of being stopped by police in an unbiased world. For example, a department collecting data only on traffic stops would, ideally, want to compare the demographics of those stopped with the demographics of those at risk of a stop, taking into consideration numerous factors, including, but not limited to, driving quantity, driving behavior, vehicle condition, and police presence. In an ideal world, we would have this information for each type of stop (e.g., red-light violation, speeding violation).

Clearly, this information is not available. Thus we create "standards" for these ideal groups. Hypothetically, if an agency wanted to know if the number of recorded traffic stops of African-Americans in a specific area was potentially too high, it would want to know the probability of the average African-American in that area's being stopped for a traffic violation (based on such objective factors as driving quantity, driving behavior, and enforcement level and type in the area). Unfortunately, departments may have information regarding only the percentage of African-Americans of driving age who *live* in the area. This comparison group is clearly less useful than the kind of "at risk" group we would like to have for analysis.

Below we describe the various standards that have been used to analyze data collected to address "racial profiling," and the limitations of each. *PERF project staff determined that there are not as yet satisfactory "best practices" in the realm of data interpretation and analysis, and thus do not make specific recommendations regarding ideal comparison groups. However, due to this deficiency in the field—and with additional funding from the Office of Community Oriented Policing Services—PERF is implementing a project that will produce such recommendations.* Specifically, PERF staff will join with experts around the country to develop guidelines for departments in this area. Pending the completion of this work, we share below some of the key issues that departments should consider in developing comparison groups that serve as "standards" for our ideal.

Standards departments have used can be categorized by whether they are based on information that is external or internal to the agency. External standards include those based on existing data, such as census data, or on new data, such as that provided by observing vehicles on the road. An internal-standard system is analogous to an early warning system in that officers, units and so forth are matched and compared with one another. (For instance, vehicle stop data for officers assigned to a particular area on a particular shift are compared.)

## EXTERNAL STANDARDS: EXISTING DATA

Most jurisdictions that have begun to analyze their data have relied on external standards developed from existing data. Below we summarize some of the standards that have been used, their positive and negative features and, where applicable, suggestions for refinement.

### Jurisdiction Residents, Based on Census Data

A number of departments around the nation have compared their vehicle stop data against census data. That is, these jurisdictions have compared the breakdown of people stopped, by race and ethnicity, with the race and ethnicity of their residents. The census data are valuable because they are easily accessible and can be broken down by small geographic units within a jurisdiction. The drawback of census data is that they do not necessarily represent people at risk of law enforcement intervention. Instead, they reveal only who lives in the jurisdiction.

To improve on these data and develop a better comparison group, agencies should

- access the most recent census data;
- include residency (as defined by the census) as one element on data collection forms;
- use the census data only for people of driving age;
- adjust the census data for vehicle ownership or driving behavior by race/ethnicity, using census information or the National Personal Transportation Survey,[17] respectively; and
- use census tract information to conduct comparisons within the jurisdiction's geographic units (if possible), such as those that correspond with precincts or other service areas.[18]

*People With Driver's Licenses*
In analyzing North Carolina Highway Patrol data, Zingraff et al.[19] used information regarding driver's licenses issued in the state. In most states, data on driver's license holders are available to the police and can be broken down by specific geo-

---

[17] See www.bts.gov/ntda/npts, as reported by Harris (1999b). For instance, this survey reported that "African-Americans comprise 11.8 percent of all households, but account for 35.1 percent of households without a vehicle" (p. 7).

[18] [This would involve, for instance, comparing the demographics of those stopped within a particular precinct or beat with the demographics of those who live there.

[19] Zingraff et al. (2000), "Evaluating North Carolina State Highway Patrol Data: Citations, Warnings and Searches in 1998," report submitted to North Carolina Department of Crime Control and Public Safety and North Carolina State Highway Patrol, Nov. 1.

graphic units. This information is superior to *unadjusted* census data because it moves us closer to assessing who is on the road and, thus, at risk of being stopped. These data, however, do not provide for a true comparison group in that they do not provide for differential law enforcement deployment on the roads (e.g., "hot spot" enforcement), do not provide for variations in driving behavior in terms of either quantity or quality (e.g., aggressive drivers are more likely to be stopped), and do not provide any information for purposes of assessing who might be at risk for an investigatory (as opposed to traffic) stop. Information on driver's licenses held within geographic units does not provide for the fact that people who live outside of the area are driving on the roads[20] (although collecting information on citizen residence—as recommended earlier—can mitigate this concern). Further, this source does not provide us with information for assessing the risk of pedestrians being stopped.

*People Involved in Vehicle Accidents*
Another group against which stop data demographics can be compared are people who have been involved in vehicle accidents. A major advantage of this comparison information over census and driver's license data is that it provides a measure of poor driving behavior. This information is also available within the police department, and includes both residents and nonresidents who are on the roads. A significant drawback is that people who have vehicle accidents (that get reported to police) do not accurately represent people who are at risk of being stopped for traffic violations or investigatory reasons. For instance, some people are involved in accidents through no fault of their own, and some very poor drivers may never get into accidents. Further, in some jurisdictions, race/ethnicity is not included among information regarding accidents.

---

[20] Zingraff et al. (2000) used residence information from a sample of citations to develop measures of the extent to which drivers licensed in one area drove in another.

*People Arrested (Uniform Crime Reports Data)*
Some jurisdictions have compared their stop data by race/ethnicity with their Uniform Crime Reports (UCR) arrest data by race/ethnicity. These are unacceptable comparison data for several reasons. First, arrest data do not measure actual crimes. These data are very much dictated by enforcement behavior (for instance, arrest data may reflect a department's focus on particular crimes or geographic areas). Second, if officers are demonstrating bias in their stops, it is likely they are also demonstrating bias in their arrests. Third, even if arrests *were* a satisfactory indicator of criminal behavior, criminal behavior is not satisfactory in indicating what puts a person at risk for traffic and/or investigatory stops, which is what we are trying to estimate. Agencies that can generate information on "race of known suspects" can partially address the first caveat above—regarding enforcement behavior's influence on UCR data—but still should be quite cautious in using this measure to create a comparison group for people stopped in their vehicles.

**External Standards: New Data**
Data collected through researchers' observations of drivers have produced additional external standards for some studies. For instance, Lamberth[21] conducted several types of observations of drivers on the New Jersey Turnpike. In one procedure, researchers counted cars on the road at various locations and times, and tabulated race/ethnicity of drivers. In another, more sophisticated, procedure, researchers conducted "rolling surveys" in which they drove five miles over the speed limit and separately tabulated the race/ethnicity of the drivers they passed and of the drivers who passed them.

These observational data can provide valuable standards in that they are better for estimating the race/ethnicity of people

---

[21] Report of Dr. John Lamberth, plaintiff's expert, "Revised Statistical Analysis of the Incidence of Police Stops and Arrests of Black Drivers/Travelers on the New Jersey Turnpike Between Exits or Interchanges 1 and 3 From the Years 1988 Through 1991," *State of New Jersey v. Pedro Soto*, 734 A. 2d 350 (N.J. Super. Ct. Law. Div. 1996).

at risk for being stopped. One drawback is that they allow for assessments only of certain types of traffic violations (e.g., speeding, red-light violations) that may not generalize to all traffic violations. Also, it may be difficult for observers to accurately discern race, particularly at night. Further, they do not provide risk assessment data for vehicle or pedestrian stops that are not based on traffic violations (e.g., for investigatory stops based on suspicious activities). Most important, however, are the practical drawbacks of using such measures. They have been used primarily for data analysis for state highway patrols and, indeed, are most conducive to assessments of a limited number of high-volume roads. Applying these measures to urban areas requires sophisticated sampling to select roads and time periods for data collection, to ensure the data are representative. Resources are required for both the design and the data collection through observation. These drawbacks noted, it's also important to report that social scientists across the country are striving to develop cost-effective methods for implementing these techniques in urban and rural jurisdictions.

**Internal Standards**

A system based on internal standards involves analyzing stop data to compare officers with other officers, units with other units, geographic areas with other geographic areas, and so forth. Critically important, these comparisons are made within "matched" sets (of officers, units, etc.) to "control" for circumstances and context. For example, officers working the same shift in the same district could be compared with one another. Districts with similar demographics, criminal activity and traffic activity could be compared. Analyses could also compare officers, units and areas over time to document trends and patterns. These analyses identify "outliers," that is, officers, units or districts that seem to intervene with racial/ethnic minorities at higher rates than their matched counterparts do. Identifying these outliers would initiate a more comprehensive inquiry into circumstances and context that could result in no action if an officer's actions are justified, or disciplinary measures (which could include counseling and retraining) if the officer's actions are unjustified.

A major benefit of this type of system is that it can provide for strong comparison groups for analyzing and interpreting data. Yet systems involving internal comparisons cannot, on their own, provide an assessment of racially biased policing at the *department level*. That is, a system that, in effect, compares the department with itself could not determine that an entire department was engaged in racially biased policing. This drawback, however, can easily be remedied by combining internal and external standards into a comprehensive analysis plan.

### Independent Analysts
Data collection is both a social science and a political endeavor. Thus, an agency must attend to both social science and political objectives in developing an analysis plan. Above we set forth some of the social science considerations; however, an agency could use high-quality social science to conduct their analysis, but lose in the political arena because the jurisdiction's citizens do not consider an internally conducted analysis to be credible. Many agencies across the country have recognized that conducting analysis wholly internal to the agency can make the results appear suspect, and thus have obtained the assistance of independent analysts.

*Recommendation: Agencies should obtain independent researchers' assistance for analyzing their racial bias data.*

The analyst(s) should be trained in social science methods and have general knowledge of law enforcement, as well as demonstrated knowledge of the specific issues associated with analyzing police detention/stop data. Capable analysts are most likely to be associated with a college/university or independent research firm. If feasible, the researcher(s) should work in conjunction with a police-citizen task force.

### Police-Citizen Development and Implementation
Citizens and police department personnel of all ranks should be represented in developing and implementing the data collection and analysis system. The police-citizen task forces recommended

in Chapter 7 should help in deciding whether to adopt a system and could be involved in design and implementation. Alternatively, a subcommittee might take on the extensive tasks associated with data collection and analysis, working with an independent social science researcher and the department's research and legal staff.

The police-citizen group should advise the agency executive, and the executive should set clear parameters for the group regarding the type of input being sought. (For instance, if the executive has certain nonnegotiable ideas about the data collection, he or she should share these early on in the process.) The police-citizen group could potentially be charged with all aspects of developing the data collection and analysis protocol, including specifying the activities to collect data on, how to collect the data, and what data elements and coding to use; and maybe even developing/selecting a comparison group. Resources for their decision-making on data collection and analysis should include this chapter.

## HOW TO GET STARTED

Having outlined some suggestions for a data collection protocol, we set forth some of the early steps for getting started.

- Unless mandated, decide, with citizen input, whether data collection should be one component of the jurisdiction's overall response to racially biased policing and the perceptions thereof.
- Communicate with agency personnel as soon as a decision is made to start collecting data. The executive should provide a rationale for data collection and address anticipated concerns.
- Set up a process for listening to personnel's concerns, and have personnel develop constructive ways to address them.
- Develop a police-citizen group to serve in an advisory capacity.
- Develop the data collection and analysis protocol. Ensure the interpretations will be responsible, based on sound methodology and analysis.

- Field-test the data collection system for three to six months, and use that test to make modifications before implementing the system jurisdictionwide.

## CONCLUSION

Data collection can be part of a police response to racially biased policing and the perceptions of its practice. As we have reiterated throughout this report, however, it should not be considered the panacea nor the only way that an agency can be accountable on and responsive to this critical issue. In developing a comprehensive response, an agency executive should work with citizen leaders to consider response protocols for accountability and supervision; policies to reduce biased policing; recruitment and hiring; training and education; community outreach; and data collection. Agency executives working cooperatively with their citizens will know best how to develop a multi-faceted response tailored to the needs of the jurisdiction that reflects the interdependence of the various solutions. They should consider, for example, the need for policy adoption to be supported by strong training; how recruitment can be facilitated by community outreach; and the need for hiring objectives to be reinforced through training and supervision. To help police and communities keep abreast of the rapid advances being made in this area, PERF will continue to develop the racially biased policing project on the PERF website (www.policeforum.org), adding new ideas, articles, model policies and protocols and other resources as they come to our attention.

While this report does not provide all the answers to racially biased policing problems, we hope that it has outlined the relevant issues and provided sufficient guidance for police and communities to work more productively together to address this critical concern.

# References

Albrecht, S., and M. Green (1977). "Attitudes Toward the Police and the Larger Attitude Complex." *Criminology* 15(1):67–86.

Alpert, G., and R. Dunham (1997). *The Force Factor: Measuring Police Use of Force Relative to Suspect Resistance.* Washington, D.C.: Police Executive Research Forum.

Block, R. (1971). "Fear of Crime and Fear of the Police." *Social Problems* 19:91–100.

*Brinegar v. United States* (1949) (338 U.S. 160).

Browning, S., F. Cullen, L. Cao, R. Kopache, and T. Stevenson (1994). "Race and Getting Hassled by the Police." *Police Studies* 17:1–11.

Bureau of Justice Statistics (2001). *Contacts Between Police and the Public: Findings From the 1999 National Survey.* Washington, D.C.: U.S. Department of Justice.

Carter, D., and A. Bannister (2001). "Racial Profiling: A Case Study of the Lansing, Michigan, Police Department." Paper presented at the Annual Meeting of the Academy of Criminal Justice Sciences, Washington, D.C., Apr. 4.

Carter, D., and A. Sapp (1991). *Police Education and Minority Recruitment: The Impact of a College Requirement.* Washington, D.C.: Police Executive Research Forum.

Cohen, J., J. Lennon, and R. Wasserman. (2000). *Eliminating Racial Profiling: A Third Way Approach.* Washington, D.C.: Progressive Policy Institute.

Cohn, E. (1996). "The Citizen Police Academy: A Recipe for Improving Police-Community Relations." *Journal of Criminal Justice* 24(3):265–271.

Cole, D. (1999). "The Color of Justice: Courts Are Protecting, Rather Than Helping To End, Racial Profiling by Police." *The Nation* 269(2):12–15.

Crew, J. (1999). "Community Policing vs. Policing the Community." *California Association of Human Relations Organizations* (February/March). www.cahro.org/html/policingthecomm.html

Davis, R. (1999). *Respectful and Effective Policing: Two Examples in the South Bronx.* New York: Vera Institute of Justice.

Decker, S. (1981). "Citizen Attitudes Toward the Police: A Review of Past Findings and Suggestions for Future Policy. *Journal of Police Science and Administration* 9(1):80–87.

Dunham, R., and G. Alpert (1988). "Neighborhood Differences in Attitudes Toward Policing: Evidence for a Mixed-Strategy Model of Policing in a Multi-Ethnic Setting." *Journal of Criminal Law and Criminology* 79(2):504–523.

Flanagan, T., and M. Vaughn (1996). "Public Opinion About Police Abuse of Force." In W. Geller and H. Toch (eds.), *Police Violence.* New Haven, Conn.: Yale University Press.

Geller, W., and M. Scott (1992). *Deadly Force: What We Know— A Practitioner's Desk Reference on Police-Involved Shootings.* Washington, D.C.: Police Executive Research Forum.

Harris, D. (1999a). *Driving While Black: Racial Profiling on Our Nation's Highways.* Washington, D.C.: American Civil Liberties Union.

——— (1999b). "The Stories, the Statistics and the Law: Why Driving While Black Matters." *Minnesota Law Review* 84(265):1–45.

——— (1997). "'Driving While Black' and All Other Offenses: The Supreme Court and Pretextual Traffic Stops." *Journal of Criminal Law and Criminology* 87:544–582.

——— (1996). "Superman's X-Ray Vision and the Fourth Amendment: The New Gun Detection Technology." *Temple Law Review* 69(1):1–60.

——— (1994). "Factors for Reasonable Suspicion: When Black and Poor Means Stopped and Frisked." *Indiana Law Journal* 69:659–688.

Hooper, M. (1988). "The Relationship of College Education to Police Officer Job Performance." Ph.D. diss. Claremont, Calif.: Claremont Graduate School.

International Association of Chiefs of Police (n.d.). "Sample Professional Traffic Stops Policy and Procedure." www.theiacp.org

——— (2001). "Traffic Stops and Data Collection." Unpublished Statement of the Board of Directors.

——— (1999). "Incorporation of Racial Background as a Data Element on Driver's Licenses." Resolution adopted at the 106th Annual Conference, Charlotte, N.C., Nov. 3.

——— (1999). "Recommendations from the First IACP Forum on Professional Traffic Stops." Apr. 6.

Kelling, G., and C. Coles (1996). *Fixing Broken Windows: Restoring Order and Reducing Crime in Our Communities.* New York: Free Press.

Kennedy, R. (1997). *Race, Crime and the Law.* New York: Pantheon Books.

Knowles, J., and N. Persico (2001). "Racial Bias in Motor Vehicle Searches: Theory and Evidence." *Journal of Political Economy* 109(1):203–229.

Kocieniewski, D. (2000). "New Jersey Argues That the U.S. Wrote the Book on Race Profiling." *New York Times,* Nov. 29.

Lamberth, J. (1996). "Revised Statistical Analysis of the Incidence of Police Stops and Arrests of Black Drivers/Travelers on the New Jersey Turnpike Between Exits or Interchanges 1 and 3 From the Years 1988 Through 1991." Plaintiff's expert's report in *State of New Jersey v. Pedro Soto* (734 A. 2d 350) (N.J. Super. Ct. Law Div.).

Lundman, R. (1994). "Demeanor or Crime? The Midwest City Police-Citizen Encounters Study." *Criminology* 32(4):631–656.

Maclin, T. (1998a). "Race and the Fourth Amendment." *Vanderbilt Law Review* 51(2):333–393.

——— (1998b). "Terry v. Ohio's Fourth Amendment Legacy: Black Men and Police Discretion." *St. John's Law Review* 72(3/4):1271–1321.

Madden, B. (1990). "The Police and Higher Education: A Study of the Relationship Between Higher Education and Police Officer Performance." Master's thesis. Louisville, Ky.: University of Louisville.

Matthews, R. (1992). "Replacing 'Broken Windows': Crime, Incivilities and Urban Change." In R. Matthews and J. Young (eds.), *Issues in Realist Criminology*. London: Sage Publications.

Meehan, A., and M. Ponder (2000). "Race and Place: The Ecology of Racial Profiling African-American Motorists." Unpublished manuscript. Rochester, Mich.: Oakland University.

Meeks, K. (2000). *Driving While Black: What To Do if You Are a Victim of Racial Profiling*. New York: Broadway Books.

Mertens, W., J. Guy and D. Jeon (1996). "Memorandum in Support of Plaintiffs' Motion for Enforcement of Settlement Agreement and for Further Relief." *Wilkins v. Maryland State Police* (CCB-93-468).

National Highway Traffic Safety Administration (2000). *Strengthening the Citizen and Law Enforcement Partnership at the Traffic Stop: Professionalism Is a Two-Way Street. Building Bridges to the Community...One Traffic Stop at a Time.* Washington, D.C.: U.S. Department of Transportation.

Newport, F. (1999). "Racial Profiling Is Seen as Widespread, Particularly Among Young Black Men." Gallup News Agency, Dec. 9. http://www.gallup.com/poll/releases/pr991209.asp

Norris, C., N. Fielding, C. Kemp, and J. Fielding (1992). "Black and Blue: An Analysis of the Influence of Race on Being Stopped by the Police." *British Journal of Sociology* 43(2):207–224.

Peak, K., R. Glensor and R. Bradshaw (1992). "Improving Citizen Perceptions of the Police: 'Back to the Basics' With a Community Policing Strategy." *Journal of Criminal Justice* 20:25–40.

"Profiling Furor Prompts Traffic-Stop Data Collection" (1999). *Law Enforcement News* 25(519):5.

"Racial Profiling: A Law Enforcement Nemesis" (1999). *Police Magazine* (November): 38–39.

Ramirez, D., J. McDevitt and A. Farrell (2000). *A Resource Guide on Racial Profiling Data Collection Systems: Promising Practices and Lessons Learned*. Washington, D.C.: U.S. Department of Justice.

Reaves, B., and A. Goldberg (1999). *Law Enforcement Management and Administrative Statistics, 1997: Data for Individual*

*State and Local Agencies With 100 or More Officers.* Washington, D.C.: U.S. Department of Justice, Bureau of Justice Statistics.

Ricigliano, R., T. Johnson and A. Chasen (1999). "Problems Without a Process: Using an Action Dialogue To Manage Racial Tensions." *Harvard Negotiation Law Review* 4:83–114.

Russell, K. (1999). "'Driving While Black': Corollary Phenomena and Collateral Consequences." *Boston College Law Review* 40(717):1–12.

———— (1998). *The Color of Crime: Racial Hoaxes, White Fear, Black Protectionism, Police Harassment, and Other Macroaggressions.* New York: New York University Press.

Saad, L., and L. McAneney (1995). "Black Americans See Little Justice for Themselves." *The Gallup Poll Monthly* (March):32–35.

San Diego Police Department (2000). "Vehicle Stop Study, Mid-Year Report," Sept. 21.

Sauls, J. (1989). "Traffic Stops, Police Power Under the Fourth Amendment." *FBI Law Enforcement Bulletin* (September):26–31.

Sigelman, L., S. Welch, T. Bledsoe, and M. Combs (1997). "Police Brutality and Public Perceptions of Racial Discrimination: A Tale of Two Beatings." *Political Research Quarterly* 50(4):777–791.

Skolnick, J. (1966). *Justice Without Trial.* New York: John Wiley and Sons.

Smith, D., C. Visher and L. Davidson (1984). "Equity and Discretionary Justice: The Influence of Race on Police Arrest Decisions." *The Journal of Criminal Law and Criminology* 75(1):234–249.

Son, I., M. Davis and D. Rome (1998). "Race and Its Effect on Police Officers' Perceptions of Misconduct." *Journal of Criminal Justice* 26(1):21–28.

Spitzer, E. (1999). The New York City Police Department's 'Stop and Frisk' Practices. New York: Attorney General of New York.

*State of Alabama v. White* (1990) (496 U.S. 325).

State of New Jersey (1999). "Interim Report of the State Police Review Team Regarding Allegations of Racial Profiling," Apr. 20.

State of New Jersey (1999). "Final Report of the State Police Review Team," July 2.

State of Wisconsin (2000). *Governor's Task Force on Racial Profiling Report.*

Thompson, A. (1999). "Stopping the Usual Suspects: Race and the Fourth Amendment." *New York University Law School* 74: 956–1013.

Tuch, S., and R. Weutzerm (1997). "The Pools—Trends, Racial Differences in Attitudes Toward the Police." *Public Opinion Quarterly* 61:642–663.

*United States v. Brignoni-Ponce* (1975) (422 U.S. 873).

*United States v. Montero Camargo* (2000) (208 F. 3d 1122, 9th Cir.).

U.S. Department of Justice (2001). *Principles for Promoting Police Integrity: Examples of Promising Police Practices and Policies.* Washington, D.C.: U.S. Department of Justice.

—— (2000a). *Conducting Complete Traffic Stops: A Community Crash and Crime Reduction Effort.* Washington, D.C.: U.S. Department of Justice.

—— (2000b). *National Race Relations Symposium: Building Peaceful Communities.* Washington, D.C.: U.S. Department of Justice.

—— (1999). "Attorney General's Conference: Strengthening Police-Community Relationships—Summary Report." Washington, D.C.: U.S. Department of Justice.

U.S. General Accounting Office (2000). "Racial Profiling: Limited Data Available on Motorist Stops." Report submitted to the Hon. James E. Clyburn, Chairman, Congressional Black Caucus, March.

Walker, S. (forthcoming). "Searching for the Denominator: Problems With Police Traffic Stop Data and an Early Warning System Solution." *Journal of Research and Policy.*

—— (2001). *Police Accountability: The Role of Citizen Oversight.* New York: Wadsworth Publishing Co.

—— (2000) (with a response by R. Myers). *Police Interactions With Racial and Ethnic Minorities: Resolving the Contradictions Between Allegations and Evidence.* Washington, D.C.: Police Executive Research Forum.

—— (1995). *Citizen Review Resource Manual.* Washington, D.C.: Police Executive Research Forum.

Walker, S., C. Spohn and M. DeLone (2000). *The Color of Justice: Race, Ethnicity and Crime in America.* Second Edition. New York: Wadsworth Publishing Co.

Weitzer, R. (2000a). "Racialized Policing: Residents' Perceptions in Three Neighborhoods." *Law and Society Review* 34(1):129–155.

——— (2000b). "White, Black or Blue Cops? Race and Assessments of Police Officers." *Journal of Criminal Justice* 28:313–324.

——— (1999). "Citizens' Perceptions of Police Misconduct: Race and Neighborhood Context." *Justice Quarterly* 16(4):819–846.

Weitzer, R., and S. Tuch (1999). "Race, Class and Perceptions of Discrimination by the Police." *Crime and Delinquency* 45(4):494–507.

*Whren et al. v. United States* (1996) (517 U.S. 806).

Wolfskill, J. (1989). "Higher Education and Police Performance." Ph.D. diss. Lawrence, Kan.: University of Kansas.

Worden, R., and R. Shepard (1996). "Demeanor, Crime and Police Behavior: A Reexamination of the Police Services Study Data." *Criminology* 34(1):83–105.

Zingraff, M., M. Mason, W. Smith, D. Tomaskovic-Devey, P. Warren, H. McMurray, and R. Fenlon (2000). "Evaluating North Carolina State Highway Patrol Data: Citations, Warnings and Searches in 1998." Report submitted to North Carolina Department of Crime Control and Public Safety and North Carolina State Highway, Nov. 1.

# About the Authors

**Lorie Fridell**

Lorie Fridell is the Director of Research at PERF. Prior to joining PERF in August 1999, Fridell was an Associate Professor of Criminology and Criminal Justice at Florida State University. She completed her Bachelors degree in psychology at Linfield College in McMinnville, Oregon, and both her Masters and Ph.D. in Social Ecology at the University of Southern California at Irvine. Fridell has conducted research on such law enforcement topics as deadly force, less than lethal force, complaints of excessive force, felonious killings of police officers, and community policing. In addition to articles and chapters on these topics, she co-authored, with Tony Pate, a two-volume report entitled *Police Use of Force: Official Reports, Citizen Complaints and Legal Consequences* and co-authored with Geoff Alpert *Police Vehicles and Firearms: Instruments of Deadly Force.*

**Robert Lunney**

Robert Lunney concluded a 44-year career in police and protective services in March 1997, with all active service in Canada. He is the former Chief of Peel Regional Police (1990 to1997), Commissioner of Protection Parks and Culture, Winnipeg (1987 to1990), Chief of Police, City of Edmonton (1974 to1987) and a retired Superintendent from the Royal Canadian Mounted Police where he served for 21 years. He is a Past President of Canadian Association of Chiefs of Police, a Life Member of the International Association of Chiefs of Police (IACP) and a PERF member since 1982. In 1995 he was decorated with the PERF Leadership Award for progressive policing practices. Currently he works as a consultant based in Toronto, Canada.

**Drew Diamond**
Drew Diamond is a Deputy Director of Research at PERF. Prior to that he completed 22 years of service with the Tulsa Police Department and served as Chief from October 1987 until his retirement in November 1991. He was an employee of the FBI until he entered the U.S. Army and became an Agent in the Army Criminal Investigations Command. He is a graduate of Northeastern Oklahoma State University, the 116th Session of the FBI National Academy and the 12th Session of the FBI National Executive Institute. Mr. Diamond has directed several large community policing projects for PERF, including Weed and Seed; Urban and Rural Neighborhood-Oriented Policing; Community Policing in Public Housing; Drug-Impacted Small Jurisdictions; Improving Police Response to People with Mental Illness; and a project for the Department of Justice, Office of Violence Against Women, to address domestic violence, sexual assault and stalking from a community-policing perspective.

**Bruce Kubu**
Bruce Kubu is a Research Associate at PERF. He is responsible for managing several research projects. His specific duties include survey development, refinement, and administration; data collection and analysis and report generation. Prior to joining PERF in 1999, Mr. Kubu spent three years with the Washington/Baltimore High Intensity Drug Trafficking Area (W/B HIDTA). His primary duties included functioning as a liaison between W/B HIDTA and the criminal justice and treatment administrators within the Washington/Baltimore corridor. He was also responsible for managing data collection, data analysis and report generation for the project. Mr. Kubu received his Masters in criminology from the University of Maryland in May 1995.

**Michael Scott**
Michael Scott is an independent police research and management consultant based in Savannah, Georgia. He was recently a Visiting Fellow with the U.S. Department of Justice, Office of Community Oriented Police Services. Scott was formerly the chief of police of the Lauderhill, Fla. Police Department, having founded that municipal police department in 1994. Prior to that he was the

Special Assistant to the Chief of Police of the St. Louis Metropolitan Police Department where he guided the implementation of problem-oriented policing. He has served as the Director of Administration for the Fort Pierce, Fla. Police Department, a Senior Researcher at the Police Executive Research Forum, the Legal Assistant to the Police Commissioner of the New York City Police Department, and a police officer in the Madison, Wisc. Police Department. He has also been a research assistant to Professor Herman Goldstein at the University of Wisconsin. Mr. Scott was the 1996 recipient of the Police Executive Research Forum's Gary P. Hayes Award for leadership in improving police service. Mr. Scott holds a J.D. from the Harvard Law School and a B.A. from the University of Wisconsin-Madison. Among other publications, he is one of the authors of the forthcoming *Problem-Oriented Guides for Police* series, the author of *Problem-Oriented Policing: Reflections on the First 20 Years* and *Managing for Success: A Police Chief's Survival Guide*, and co-author of *Tackling Crime and Other Public-Safety Problems: Case Studies in Problem Solving* and *Deadly Force: What We Know. A Practitioner's Desk Reference to Police-Involved Shootings in the United States*.

### Colleen B. Laing

Ms. Laing is a consultant and researcher on criminal justice and human services issues. She lives in Seattle, Washington, working with regional and national clients on criminal justice, human services, and workforce issues. Ms. Laing has been a Fellow with the Office of Community Oriented Policing Services (COPS Office) at the U.S. Department of Justice, a Research Analyst and Program Manager with the Seattle Police Department, a Researcher with the King County Community Services Division, a Presidential Management Intern and Management Analyst with the U.S. Department of Health and Human Services' Administration for Children and Families, and a legislative office staff member in the Washington State House of Representatives and the U.S. House of Representatives. Ms. Laing earned a Bachelor of Sciences degree from Santa Clara University and holds a Masters degree in Public Administration, having graduated with honors from the University of Southern California's Washington, D.C. Public Affairs Center.

# About the Office of Community Oriented Policing Services (COPS) U.S. Department of Justice

The Office of Community Oriented Policing Services (COPS) was created in 1994 and has the unique mission to serve the needs of state and local law enforcement. The COPS Office is an innovative agency that has been the driving force in advancing the concept of community policing through the creation of locally driven problem-solving strategies and police-community partnerships. COPS is responsible for one of the greatest infusions of resources into state and local law enforcement in our nation's history.

Since 1994, COPS has invested $7.5 billion to add community policing officers to the nation's streets, enhance crime fighting technology, support crime prevention initiatives, and advance community policing nationwide. COPS funding has furthered the advancement of community policing through community policing innovation conferences, the development of model practices, pilot community policing programs, and applied research and evaluation initiatives. COPS has also positioned itself to respond directly to emerging law enforcement needs. Examples include working in partnership with departments to enhance police integrity, promoting safe schools, and combating the methamphetamine drug problem.

The COPS Office has made substantial investments in law enforcement training. COPS created a national network of training institutes that has revolutionized law enforcement training, and also supports the advancement of community policing strategies through the national training delivery system provided by the Community Policing Consortium. Furthermore, COPS has made a major investment in research which makes possible the growing body of substantive knowledge covering all aspects of community policing.

These substantial investments have produced a significant community policing infrastructure across the country as evidenced by the fact that more than two-thirds of the nation's law enforcement agencies have sought COPS grants and were awarded funding. The COPS Office continues to respond proactively by providing critical resources, training, and technical assistance to help state and local law enforcement implement innovative and effective community policing strategies.

# About PERF

The Police Executive Research Forum (PERF) is a national professional association of chief executives of large city, county and state law enforcement agencies. PERF's objective is to improve the delivery of police services and the effectiveness of crime control through several means:

- the exercise of strong national leadership,
- the public debate of police and criminal issues,
- the development of research and policy, and
- the provision of vital management and leadership services to police agencies.

PERF members are selected on the basis of their commitment to PERF's objectives and principles. PERF operates under the following tenets:

- Research, experimentation and exchange of ideas through public discussion and debate are paths for the development of a comprehensive body of knowledge about policing.
- Substantial and purposeful academic study is a prerequisite for acquiring, understanding and adding to that body of knowledge.
- Maintenance of the highest standards of ethics and integrity is imperative in the improvement of policing.
- The police must, within the limits of the law, be responsible and accountable to citizens as the ultimate source of police authority.
- The principles embodied in the Constitution are the foundation of policing.

# Related PERF Titles

*And Justice for All: Understanding and Controlling Police Abuse of Force*

*Citizen Involvement: How Community Factors Affect Progressive Policing*

*Citizen Review Resource Manual*

*Deadly Force: What We Know—A Practitioner's Desk Reference on Police-Involved Shootings*

*Drug Enforcement in Minority Communities: The Minneapolis Police Department, 1985-1990*

*Force Factor: Measuring Police Use of Force relative to Suspect Resistance*

*Police Education and Minority Recruitment: The Impact of a College Requirement*

*Police Interactions with Racial and Ethnic Minorities: Resolving the Contradictions Between Allegations and Evidence*

*Policing a Multicultural Community*

*Why Police Organizations Change: A Study of Community-Oriented Policing*

PERF also has many publications on community problem solving, evaluating police agencies and practices and other materials used for promotion exams, training and university classes. For a free catalog or more information, call toll-free to 1-888-202-4563. PERF's online bookstore can be found at www.policeforum.org on the Publications section of the Website.